Come and See

Previous books by Ronald P. Byars

*Christian Worship:
Glorifying and Enjoying God*

*The Future of Protestant Worship:
Beyond the Worship Wars*

*The Bread of Life:
A Guide to the Lord's Supper for Presbyterians*

*Lift Your Hearts on High:
Eucharistic Prayer in the Reformed Tradition*

*What Language Shall I Borrow?
The Bible and Christian Worship*

The Sacraments in Biblical Perspective

Come and See

Presbyterian Congregations Celebrating Weekly Communion

Ronald P. Byars

CASCADE *Books* • Eugene, Oregon

COME AND SEE
Presbyterian Congregations Celebrating Weekly Communion

Copyright © 2014 Ronald P. Byars. All rights reserved. Except for brief quotations in critical publications or reviews, no part of this book may be reproduced in any manner without prior written permission from the publisher. Write: Permissions, Wipf and Stock Publishers, 199 W. 8th Ave., Suite 3, Eugene, OR 97401.

Cascade Books
An Imprint of Wipf and Stock Publishers
199 W. 8th Ave., Suite 3
Eugene, OR 97401

www.wipfandstock.com

ISBN 13: 978-1-62032-589-6

Cataloguing-in-Publication data:

Byars, Ronald P.

    Come and see : Presbyterian congregations celebrating weekly communion / Ronald P. Byars ; with a Foreword by John D. Witvliet.

    xvi + 134 pp. ; 23 cm. Includes bibliographical references and index.

    ISBN 13: 978-1-62032-589-6

    1. Lord's Supper—Presbyterian Church. 2. Lord's Supper—Frequency of communion. 3. Parishes—United States—Case studies. I. Witvliet, John D. II. Title.

BX9189 .C5. B93 2014

Manufactured in the U.S.A.

Unless otherwise noted, the Scripture quotations in this publication are from the New Revised Standard Version of the Bible, copyright © 1989 by the Division of Christian Education of the National Council of Churches of Christ in the U.S.A.

This book is dedicated to pastoral colleagues with whom I served at Second Presbyterian Church, Lexington, Kentucky or First Presbyterian Church, Birmingham, Michigan

Roy Howard

Louise Westfall

Benjamin Bishop

Contents

Foreword ix
Preface xiii
Acknowledgments xv
Abbreviations xvi

One   Come and See   1
Two   Will It Bring the Numbers Up?   26
Three   Problems, Obstacles, and Opportunities   48
Four   Introducing Change Successfully   74
Five   Where Are We Going and How Shall We Get There?   96
Six   Owning the Practice   114

Bibliography   127
Index   129

Foreword

Here is a book that belongs on many different shelves in your congregation's library. Dutiful librarians will likely place it on the worship shelf, right next to a hymnal, a service book such as the *Book of Common Worship*, and other recent titles about preaching, baptism, common prayer, and congregational song. This is a good choice. For this book is an extended testimony about the value of Lord's Supper celebrations that are both frequent and robust, full of truth and grace.

But this book also belongs on other church-library shelves. It belongs on the congregational-leadership shelf, with other books that explore the nature of a genuinely pastoral form of leadership. It belongs with books on Christian mission, as it describes how the formative dimensions of the Lord's Supper connect with soup kitchens and Trinitarian witness in a postmodern world. It belongs with books on Reformed and Presbyterian identity in an ecumenical age, as it narrates the way that ecumenical learning over the past few generations has helped Reformed and Presbyterian congregations reclaim a significant part of their own sacramental heritage. It also belongs with books that explore the use and function of Scripture in congregational life, as it describes how the Bible gives us not only commands to celebrate the Lord's Supper, but also a set of potent metaphors, images, and theological motifs that help us interpret its meaning. And someday the volume will serve well on a history shelf, offering an on-the-ground view of how the broad liturgical movement of the past two generations has affected congregational life in a remarkable variety of congregations—established and emerging, large and small, urban and rural, in north and south. This book, in other words, is a synthetic book. It unfolds a vision of sacramental public worship as an integrating focal practice, one that is webbed together with every other facet of Christian life and ministry.

This also means that for this book to gain its best hearing it will need to be studied by several kinds of people. It is a book for pastors, to be sure. Through its many anecdotes, this book offers a sustained narrative argument about the indispensable role that committed pastors play in shaping worshiping communities of full, conscious, active participation.

Foreword

But this is also a book for musicians, artists, and all others who shape public worship services. And it is also a book for any congregational taskforce, committee, or staff members with responsibilities in the areas of education, discipleship, social witness, pastoral care, or evangelism—as well as the elders, officers, board or council members who guide and support them. Lord's Supper practices are a crucial aspect of how worshipers in congregations express love not only for God but also for other members of their congregation and their neighbors. Noticing and enhancing this does not need to lead to a utilitarian view of the Lord's Supper as a means to other ends.

The true flourishing of a worshiping community happens when worship functions as an integrating practice—when the congregation's educators develop pedagogies not only to promote biblical literacy but also to deepen participation in worship; when the congregation's social justice advocates begin to perceive and then testify about the profound connection between how God feeds us at the Lord's Table and then feeds the hungry through community gardens and soup kitchens; when pastoral leaders discover that worship leadership—through prophetic preaching and priestly prayer—is the cornerstone of all effective congregational leadership. May this book serve to strengthen this integrative vision in many congregations!

Theological Education

This synthetic vision also has implications for seminaries. Even as recently as a generation ago, the vast majority of Protestant seminaries rarely had dedicated courses on the study of Christian worship. When instruction was offered, it was typically offered as a brief appendix to a preaching course. Spurred by the radically different influences of ecumenical worship renewal on the one hand, and the change sparked by post-1960s popular culture, church growth, and the charismatic movement on the other, most seminaries now have dedicated courses to help students sort out wise approaches to worship. In many places, worship is taught as a Christian practice, alongside other courses on aspects of ministry, including preaching, education, pastoral care, and evangelism. The focus in such courses is placed on how worship should be structured, the nature of liturgical leadership, and the skills necessary to shape public prayer, to choose congregational songs, and to organize the church's worship calendar. In other places, courses focus mostly on the history of Christian worship, explaining the gradual development of liturgies and the Christian year, and the historical

Foreword

origins of remarkably divergent worship traditions across the spectrum of denominations.

Astute readers of this volume will quickly see that each of these two approaches is necessary but also insufficient alone. Skill development is crucial. The capacity to lead a Lord's Supper liturgy with understanding is fundamental to the renewal of participation. Historical perspective is crucial. How else can one gain perspective on the strengths and weaknesses of our own culturally shaped perceptions and practices?

But liturgical renewal is also about so much more. It involves firm, but patient pastoral leadership. It involves imaginative, contextually appropriate pedagogy. It involves pastoral care that pays attention to the deepest needs, and not only the expressed wishes, of religious seekers and lifelong worshipers. It involves theologically perceptive preaching—preaching that challenges the implicit gnosticism of those who doubt the value of embodied practices, that invites people to perceive the stunning breadth of the Bible's own authorized interpretations of the feast of the Lord's Supper as a meal of memory, communion, and hope.

All of this makes the case that a book like this belongs in several parts of a seminary curriculum—in Bible, history, theology; in courses on worship, formation, leadership and congregational life. And the fact that the book is anecdotal and testimonial should not deter its use in seminary contexts. It belongs alongside academic treatises on the history, theology, and practice of the Lord's Supper; it belongs as a rhetorical witness to the high value of pastorally framed, on-the-ground congregational experiences, as well as to the stunning variety of congregations that compose the tapestry of North American Christianity, even within a single tradition. In fact, stories told here are precisely the kind that motivate intense, analytic, academic study.

As several cultural commentators have noted, one side effect of living in an information age is that we live in an age of specialization, atomization, and isolation. In this context, how splendid it is that gifts of God for the people of God that come to us at the Lord's Table are all about communion, mutuality, and web-like connections. And how splendid it is that the testimonies and wisdom that Ron Byars has gathered here further invite us into this integrative way of life—a life of memory, communion, and hope in Jesus Christ.

John D. Witvliet
Calvin Institute of Christian Worship
Calvin College and Calvin Theological Seminary
Grand Rapids, Michigan

Preface

Presbyterians are certainly not alone among ecclesiastical folk in being profoundly concerned about our own future. The statistics are in, and they don't look good. It is far too easy to view diminishing numbers as a signal to look for someone to blame; or, at least to try to identify some single phenomenon as the cause leading to our distress. The causes, however, are multiple and complex, much as we hate to hear that, because complexity means that there is no easy fix. Further, a closer look at what is happening to mainline and even evangelical churches leads us to understand that, whatever our own institutional faults may be, there are larger social forces in play over which we have little or no control.

Against the huge background of large-scale social change, polarization in society, and the decline of the church's public influence, it is human nature for us to be preoccupied with the close-at-hand denominational issues in which we might at least conceivably be able to exercise some control. A major one seems to emerge reliably at least once in every generation, so that every twenty or twenty-five years we find ourselves with a dispute on our hands. As uncomfortable as a quarrel makes us, our conflicts have normally been defined in dramatic terms, as though the issue at hand is clear enough that if our side should not prevail, the gospel itself would be at risk, thus obligating us to pursue what almost amounts to holy war. The result is usually defections and division.

It is certain that issues related to ordination, gender, and sexuality are serious ones that do indeed cause us to wrestle with how we understand the authority of the Bible, and what we understand the gospel to require of us. They will not be resolved easily or simply, and may very well require of all the parties more time and patience than we are accustomed to devoting to anything. The problem is particularly acute in an instant culture, in which everything from microwaved meals to electronic communication to knotty problems of economics, politics, and theology has become a right-now

Preface

affair, demanding resolution in the short term rather than over the long term.

A Storehouse of Treasures

This book is intended to suggest that our church has in its storehouse of treasures practices that, were they to be more fully deployed, have a certain healing power. The greatest of these practices is the Lord's Supper, Holy Communion. It ought not become another issue to fight about, but rather something hopeful toward which all may turn with more than casual attention and with a heightened sense of expectation. If the movement to restore the Lord's Supper to its rightful place in our practice and our affections should swell into an even larger movement than it has to date, it may very well have a far greater impact on our denominational future than how we resolve the next conflict or amend the Form of Government. Even while we wrestle with issues of gender, sexuality, ordination, and polity, we may work together across the various lines of demarcation to rediscover the gift of unity with the risen Christ and one another that the Holy Spirit manifests in the Eucharist. And discover as well that our worship can embrace new generations who have been formed differently from the children of the Enlightenment.

This book records the experience of a few pastors and congregations who are celebrating the Lord's Supper every week in at least one of their services. They offer a variety of models for how to initiate such a practice and how to incorporate it into their schedules, worship spaces, and local cultures. They are diverse yet united in their confidence that weekly Communion is biblical, Reformed, faithful, and immediately relevant to new generations. May their numbers be multiplied!

Ronald P. Byars
Professor Emeritus of Preaching and Worship
Union Presbyterian Seminary

Acknowledgments

Thanks to the General Assembly's Office of Theology and Worship, and particularly to David Gambrell and Teresa Stricklen for organizing a consultation on the liturgy in November 2011, at which encounters with several of the participants in this study stirred the desire to record their experiences with weekly Eucharist. They are the Reverends Fred R. Anderson; Charles L. Andrus; David B. Batchelder; Neal D. Presa, Moderator of the 220th General Assembly; and Thomas M. Trinidad, Vice-Moderator of the 220th General Assembly.

During the course of researching the book, it was my pleasure to interview them and several others who made substantial contributions to it, including the Reverends Sidney M. Burgess, Brant S. Copeland, Jonathan E. Carroll, Elizabeth M. Deibert; Michael C. Gehrling, T. Judson Hendrix, James H. Lee, Laura L. Mendenhall, Charles M. Mendenhall, Ryan D. Shrauner, Russell C. Sullivan, Jim Walker, Adam H. Fronczek, Corey A. Nelson, and Stephen R. Montgomery. I am grateful for these servants of Christ and the church who were so willing and gracious to reflect on their experience with me and for the whole church.

Abbreviations

BCP	*Book of Common Prayer*
BCW	*Book of Common Worship*
DW	*Directory for Worship*
ELW	*Evangelical Lutheran Worship*
LBW	*Lutheran Book of Worship*
ELCA	Evangelical Lutheran Church in America
NCD	New Church Development
PCUSA	Presbyterian Church (U.S.A.)
SLD	Service for the Lord's Day

One

Come and See

They Shall Come from East and West...

Neal Presa, pastor of the Presbyterian Church in Middlesex, New Jersey, was elected Moderator of the 220th General Assembly of the Presbyterian Church USA (PCUSA). Middlesex, a town of about fourteen thousand residents just forty-five minutes west of New York City, is a predominantly Italian-American community with a large Roman Catholic parish but also two or three large nondenominational churches nearby. While nominally Catholic for the most part, many Middlesex residents send their children to catechism but are not themselves active in the parish. Though highly churched, the ambience of the community tends to be secular.

Middlesex Presbyterians recently celebrated their fiftieth anniversary, the congregation having been chartered on Pentecost in 1962. The congregation is small, with fewer than a hundred members, about half of whom have grown up in the community while the other half are more likely to be from West Africa—Cameroon or Sierra Leone. It is not uncommon for the West African members, about half of them cradle Presbyterians, to be highly educated. If you should decide to visit Middlesex Presbyterian Church at its service on Sunday morning, you will see that the Communion Table has been prepared with Bread and Cup, and the service will lead to the meal. Is it the first Sunday of the month? Maybe. But if you come back on the second Sunday or the third, or any Sunday at all, you will find the Table prepared for you and for all the people of God.

Come and See

If you were to travel 1,767 miles west from Middlesex, you might choose to worship with Faith Presbyterian Church in Colorado Springs, whose pastor, Tom Trinidad, is Vice Moderator of the 220th General Assembly. When you hear the name Colorado Springs, your mind may turn to Focus on the Family or another evangelical organization such as the Navigators, Young Life, or Youth for Christ, all of which have offices there. A lot of people in Colorado Springs go to church, and many to very conservative churches, but it is a big city (population 660,319), and there is a large, growing and increasingly public and vocal minority report, according to the Vice Moderator. Those who do not go to church have some idea of either what they have rejected or what they think they have rejected.

When Tom Trinidad interviewed at Faith Presbyterian, the committee described the church as relatively small in a sea of megachurches and moderate in a flood of conservative expressions of Christianity. He was impressed by their directness and by their integrity. Faith Church, organized in 1955, records a membership of about two hundred, and it is growing. Worship attendance rose 13 percent in the past year, and the average age of worshipers is getting younger. At Faith, as at Middlesex Presbyterian, the Table is set every Sunday.

Faith Church no longer advertises in the yellow pages but reaches out primarily through the Internet. Their website makes it very clear that they are a PCUSA church and that worship includes weekly Communion. The sign in front of the church is equally explicit. Some newcomers come because they are committed to the PCUSA. Others are drawn by weekly Communion, including some who were accustomed to that in other denominations, but also Presbyterians and others who had been used to quarterly or monthly Communion but know they want more and have come looking for it intentionally.

Ordained PCUSA ministers, nearly all of whom have had to pass an ordination exam in Worship and Sacraments, know that the denomination's *Directory for Worship* (part of the *Book of Order*) says that "it is appropriate to celebrate the Lord's Supper as often as each Lord's Day."[1] Accordingly, the Service for the Lord's Day in the denomination's *Book of Common Worship* sets forth weekly Eucharist as the norm to which all would do well to aspire. However, although a significant number of respondents to a Sacramental Practices Survey undertaken in 2011 by the PCUSA Office of Research

---

1. W-2.4009

Services would prefer Communion every week, that practice is the exception.[2] It is still a surprise when visiting a Presbyterian church to discover a congregation that shares the meal in at least one service every Lord's Day. Even more surprising is to find a church whose only service is always a service of Word and Sacrament, like both Middlesex and Faith Churches.

And South and North . . .

And yet, in more and more congregations—from California to New York, and Alabama to Vermont (Presbyterians east and west, south and north)— are moving toward Lord's Day worship in which the Word is proclaimed in Scripture and sermon and then sealed in the Sacrament every Sunday. Harrison, in northwest Arkansas, is a town where it is more likely that the houses will have a front porch than a deck on the back. A visitor is likely to see a lot of cars with Confederate flags in this town of twelve thousand where there are seventy-six churches and a huge Wal-Mart that can swell the population to forty thousand during shopping hours. As you might expect, there is a strong Southern Baptist presence here, but the religious culture is also influenced by the Churches of Christ, who use no musical instruments in worship. When Charles ("Chip") Andrus, an Arkansas native, became pastor in 2006, First Presbyterian Church had a membership of about 280, and by 2011 it had grown by over 20 percent. No doubt it helped to have a new building, completed four months after his arrival, but Chip's commitment to deepening the worship life of the congregation mattered, too. They have been celebrating the Lord's Supper every Sunday morning for several years and continue weekly Communion even as Chip has answered another call.

Far from Harrison but closer to Middlesex is the Madison Avenue Presbyterian Church, situated on the Upper East Side in one of the wealthiest areas of New York City, but with members from all over the metro area as well as from the Tri-State Area of New Jersey, New York, and Connecticut. This is the church where a young man named Frederick Buechner heard George Buttrick preach so compellingly that it changed the direction of his life.

Since February 2002, under the leadership of its pastor, Fred Anderson, Madison Avenue Church has been celebrating the Lord's Supper weekly at both of its two morning services and at its 7:30 p.m. service

---

2. Presbyterian Church (USA) Research Services, "Sacramental Practices."

as well. Like Faith Church in Colorado Springs, Madison Avenue is experiencing growth in the number of younger members. Why? "I think a younger generation—folks right up into maybe their early forties—have a very different expectation about what worship should be," Anderson commented. Some new members are looking for a different way to worship, for a way that's less about instruction and more about the mystery of meeting Christ. "The whole notion of the Eucharist is that it is where we encounter the presence of Christ now," says Anderson. At Madison Avenue, they are celebrating adult Baptisms three, four, and five times a year, and the service of both Word and Sacrament has become a part of the congregation's identity. Young families presume that weekly Communion is simply normative.

Anderson, who served on the task force that developed the PCUSA's official *Directory for Worship*, had earlier served as pastor of Pine Street Presbyterian Church in Harrisburg, Pennsylvania, which he also led to weekly celebration of the Lord's Supper. Pine Street has been celebrating the Eucharist every Lord's Day at both of its morning services for over twenty years. When Fred Anderson left in response to a call to Madison Avenue in 1992, the Session and the Mission Review Committee at Pine Street determined that weekly Communion had become central to the spiritual nurture of the congregation as well as an important part of the congregation's identity, and further recommended that support for weekly Communion be a criterion for the selection of the next pastor. Accordingly, the person invited to be the new pastor accepted the call in part because he felt drawn by their practice of weekly Communion. Russell Sullivan, the current pastor, is the second to follow Anderson's pastorate, and he also delights in the identity of the congregation as a weekly Word and Sacrament church.

Owensboro is a small city of about fifty-eight thousand people in western Kentucky, near the Indiana border. Jonathan Carroll became pastor of First Presbyterian Church in January 2005. It is a congregation with a reputation for being highly educated, erudite and well-to-do, but as times have changed, so has the congregation, and it has become more diverse. While the congregation still includes plenty of physicians, attorneys, teachers, and college and university faculty, it has also become more blended both socially and educationally. When Jonathan Carroll became pastor, the congregation hoped to recover from a substantial loss of members in the wake of a difficult and distressful time in its life.

The Owensboro congregation was trying something new when they celebrated the Lord's Supper every Sunday in Advent 2007. After Christmas, they reverted to their traditional schedule. They planned to celebrate the Sacrament weekly again in Lent of 2008 but revisited that decision, opting instead for weekly Communion on the Sundays of Eastertide. During those weeks of celebrating the meal every Sunday, the Session engaged in serious reflection about the Sacraments, and resolved not to suspend weekly Communion at the end of the Easter season but to continue for a full liturgical year. At the end of that year, concluding at Pentecost in 2009, the Session decided to make weekly celebration permanent. Many of those who had left the congregation have returned, membership is increasing, attendance is growing, and financial support has increased as well. The congregation is completing a renovation of its building.

From Quarterly to Monthly to . . .

Many Presbyterian congregations have moved from the traditional quarterly to monthly Communion, often simply designating a specific Sunday of the month—usually the first—as Communion Sunday. Of course, while that practice provides for regularity and predictability, it is not related at all to the Christian year, so that a congregation may celebrate the meal on a first Sunday but not on the following Sunday, which may be Easter or Pentecost. When David Batchelder was pastor of the Latrobe (Pennsylvania) Presbyterian Church, that congregation combined both practices, following the suggestion of the PCUSA's first Supplemental Liturgical Resource of adding Communion in festival seasons to Communion one Sunday a month.[3] This usually means adding Sundays such as the First in Advent, the Baptism of the Lord, Easter and Pentecost, Trinity Sunday, and Christ the King. In Latrobe, they added the big occasions in the liturgical calendar but also celebrated weekly Communion every Sunday between Easter Day and Pentecost as well as on the first Sunday of each month during ordinary time, that long period that stretches over the summer and into the fall between Trinity Sunday and the Reign of Christ (Christ the King).

David Batchelder now serves the West Plano Presbyterian Church in the Dallas–Fort Worth area metroplex, a congregation that celebrates the sacred meal weekly. The West Plano church, established in 1975, had deliberately sought a pastor who would support them in sustaining and deepening their rich liturgical tradition, and David followed the call even though it led him from a larger to a smaller congregation—not a typical move.

3. Presbyterian Church (USA), *Service for the Lord's Day*.

Come and See

In 2003, when David arrived in West Plano, the public schools reported that they enrolled students from ninety-two national backgrounds. Collin County was and still is growing fast. It is, by and large, an affluent community, but one may still find people there who are struggling with homelessness. When David began his ministry, the congregation had two Sunday morning services, but attendance at the second service had begun to decline. They had been celebrating the Lord's Supper every week at the early service since the early 1990s, beginning the practice under the leadership of the congregation's third pastor, the Reverend Wes Lackey. The second service celebrated the Eucharist frequently, but not every Sunday, following the pattern of festival seasons and the odd Sundays (first, third, and sometimes fifth) during ordinary time. West Plano began a weekly celebration at both services in 2006. Having had a positive experience with a single service during the summer, and having adequate space, they chose to move to a single service in 2009, with weekly Communion.

The Edgewood Presbyterian Church is located in Homewood, the oldest suburb just south of the city of Birmingham, Alabama. Edgewood was founded in 1912 as members from two Cumberland Presbyterian churches came together to organize a congregation to be affiliated with the PCUSA, the so-called Northern church in that time decades before reunion. In the early twentieth century, Homewood was largely rural, and Edgewood was the first church of any kind to be organized there. It functioned as a community church, including people from several denominations. When the congregation called a pastor who was (so to speak) "too Presbyterian" for the Baptists, they left and started their own church. The Methodists followed soon after. With a population of about twenty-five thousand people, Homewood now has many churches, a number of them very large.

In 1978, two-thirds of the Edgewood membership followed the pastor out of the denomination and into the Presbyterian Church in America. The faithful remnant was left to pay off the mortgage on what was then a new building. After a dozen years of struggle, Sid Burgess came to be their pastor in 1990, serving another Presbyterian congregation at the same time. The remaining Edgewood members numbered around fifty. General Assembly statistics now report a membership of 218, nearly all current members having joined since 1990 from all over the Birmingham region. Those who find Edgewood and make it their church home are drawn by its relatively small size in a predominantly churched community with many congregations from which to choose. About a third of the current congregation have been lifelong Presbyterians; another third come from free-church backgrounds (Baptist, Church of Christ, and the like); the remaining third were everything from ex-Roman Catholics to folks with no church background at all. A More Light congregation, many of Edgewood's members have been attracted by its self-identification as "open-minded, open-hearted."

When Burgess arrived, they celebrated the Lord's Supper on the first Sunday of the month, but after a time added the festival days. After a few years, they added every Sunday in Easter, celebrating the presence of the risen Lord. Then they added the Sundays of Advent, then the Sundays in Lent. In about 1998, upon motion by an elder on the Session, they closed the circle and began to celebrate the Lord's Supper every week.

In a growing number of established PCUSA congregations, Communion stands alongside preaching in every Lord's Day service. Some would appropriately be described as progressive while others would be more likely to be profiled as evangelical. Still others defy easy categorization, and might be described more generally as broadly, middle-of-the-road Presbyterian. They come from backgrounds in both the former Southern and Northern churches. The move to weekly celebration is not easily linked to any single theological, geographic, or historical descriptor.

In the past half century, the number of Presbyterian congregations that celebrate the Lord's Supper only quarterly has declined significantly, while by far the greater number celebrate the meal monthly, and a large number celebrate on feast days as well as on a specific Sunday once a month. Following the latter model, some congregations, such as First Presbyterian Church in Tallahassee, led by its pastor, Brant Copeland, celebrate the Supper at least twice a month and often more; or University Presbyterian Church in Austin, Texas, led by its pastor, San Williams, which celebrates the meal every Sunday during Advent and on the Sundays of Easter and on the first and third Sundays of every month as well.

New Church Developments

Long-established congregations face challenges whenever introducing any change in eucharistic practice, whether from quarterly to monthly, or from monthly alone to adding feast days and festival seasons, or from twice a month to every week. The situation is entirely different for a New Church Development (NCD). When a new congregation is in process of organization, those who participate in the project are likely to be people who are willing to take some risks and do not expect their past church experiences to be replicated exactly as they have known them. With a new beginning, a sense of adventure is part of the package. The organizing pastor is likely to share the enthusiasm that accompanies a new beginning, and to be looking for an opportunity to lay strong foundations. This can be a good time for reexamining closely and carefully the long historical tradition of the ecumenical and Reformed church of Jesus Christ and for recovering things of value that may have been either lost or obscured. More and more often, that has meant recovering weekly Communion.

Elizabeth Deibert was the organizing pastor (and is now the pastor) of Peace Presbyterian Church in a planned suburban community called Lakewood Ranch, east of both Bradenton and Sarasota on the west coast of Florida. The community itself is about fifteen years old. When the Presbyterians came to Lakewood Ranch, the United Methodists, Baptists, Roman Catholics, Lutherans and Episcopalians were already there. The congregation began worshiping in 2006, and was chartered in 2009.

Deibert describes the Lakewood Ranch community as "very secular" and oriented toward recreation. Most of the population consists of transplants, younger retirees, and empty nesters, although there are also young families, and Peace Church is working hard to attract all of them. From its first service of worship, the congregation has been celebrating the Lord's Supper every week.

This is not the first time Deibert has served as an organizing pastor of an NCD. She and her husband, Richard Deibert, also a minister of the PCUSA, organized the Immanuel Presbyterian Church in Montgomery, Alabama, in 1990, which has also celebrated the Sacrament weekly from the beginning, continuing now for more than twenty years. Deibert is persuaded that many of the young families who are drawn to churches like Peace and Immanuel are looking for what she describes as the "mystery" that the Sacrament brings to worship. Those under the age of thirty-five, she observes, are most likely to be in search of such a service.

Mystery, readers will understand, is different from mystification. Mystery is a quality of awe, of reverence before something (or Someone) that cannot be easily packaged in a rational explanation that wraps everything up and sets it aside as settled. Mystery is experienced first and reflected upon later. It can and must be, by the nature of the case, encountered more than explained, and pondered over a lifetime. It is a matter of a meeting, of discerning or apprehending, more than a mental process. The prayer at the Table, like the Bread and Cup; like the sharing, the giving, the eating, and drinking, is part of the mystery. "I never fail to call down the Holy Spirit," Deibert declares.

Also chartered in 2009 is the New Covenant Fellowship in Austin, Texas. James Lee was on the staff of Covenant Presbyterian Church in Austin when he was asked to organize a new congregation, which began with a Bible-study group in 2004. Lee is an African American whose family of origin has always been Presbyterian. Lee is a graduate of Austin Seminary, where his teachers included the late Professor Stan Hall, whose years of teaching seminarians about Reformed worship have left a lasting legacy. When the idea of forming a new church was first conceived, it was thought that it should be African American, but the Steering Committee discerned a call to create a racially diverse, multicultural church. About 60 percent of the current members are Euro-American, while 15 percent are African, 10 percent are African American or Asian American, and Latinos number about 15 percent. Roughly 25 percent of the current members have been Presbyterians before. The remainder have come from Missionary Baptist, Southern Baptist, Methodist, Roman Catholic, Assemblies of God, or Church of Christ backgrounds; had no church affiliation; or professed no faith at all.

New Covenant Fellowship sought out a geographical base with a population that was diverse racially and primarily middle-class. For now, they worship in the Fellowship Hall of the Genesis Presbyterian Church in Austin, permitting them to reduce expenses and geographically convenient for a congregation drawn from their identified target area of the city. New Covenant Fellowship has been celebrating the Lord's Supper weekly from the beginning. Lee, like Deibert, favors the word *mystery* to describe the attraction of Communion. He believes that the prayer of Thanksgiving helps to frame the meal as one of victory, quoting the Memorial Acclamation from the Great Thanksgiving: "Christ has died. Christ is risen. Christ will come again."

"We always focus on Christian victory, the victorious Christ," Lee declared.

When asked whether he would recommend the practice of weekly Communion to another church, and particularly an African American church, Lee responded that he would. "What we would say to the African American community is that because Jesus got up, we can get up. Why celebrate the victory of Christ once a month when we could celebrate it weekly?" Both *The Presbyterian Hymnal* and its successor, *Glory to God*, as well as the hymnals of other denominations, include a triumphant hymn that lifts up the victory theme so important to Lee: "This is the feast of victory for our God. Alleluia, Alleluia, Alleluia!"

In the late 1990s, a small group of Presbyterians near Lake Travis, in the Austin area, began worshiping in their homes in a community called Lakeway, which is outside the city and far from existing Presbyterian churches. These worshipers sought the care of Westminster Church in Austin during the pastorate of Laura Mendenhall. Westminster's Session provided oversight, authorizing Baptism and the Lord's Supper for the small community and keeping records for them. When the Westminster congregation celebrated their fiftieth anniversary, they helped to raise money for the group at Lakeway. In 2007, the group was chartered as the Presbyterian Church of Lake Travis.

Mendenhall, who had left Westminster to become president of Columbia Seminary, returned to Texas after her presidency to serve as senior philanthropy consultant for the Texas Presbyterian Foundation, and in October of 2010 was named designated pastor for Lake Travis on a part-time basis. Mendenhall worked closely with her husband, Charles (Chuck) Mendenhall, parish associate at Lake Travis, who is senior development officer with Presbyterian Children's Homes and Services in Austin.

The Lake Travis Presbyterians had had two pastorates preceding the leadership of Laura and Chuck Mendenhall, but in spite of their efforts, their numbers had diminished, and the situation had become fragile. When the Mendenhalls began their work there, it was not at all clear whether the fledgling group would survive. Laura and Chuck were both asked to work part time, each giving about ten hours a week. With new leadership that brought such a depth of experience, the result has been a pronounced turnaround, and within six months the congregation bought land for a new building, which was completed in early 2013. Laura is no longer the designated pastor, but the pastor, while Chuck continues in his role as parish associate. Since the two always lead worship, they tend to be seen as co-pastors.

The Lake Travis congregation consists mostly of retired people who have moved out to be near the lake, although there are a few younger families. Most of the members have been Presbyterians, and know how Presbyterians do things. One of the two ministers to have served the congregation in formation before the arrival of the Mendenhalls had introduced the practice of weekly Communion. When Chuck and Laura began their ministry there, almost in a position of starting over, the question arose whether the congregation would continue weekly Communion. It was the local decision makers who decided to continue, and the Mendenhalls supported it. Laura, in particular, who "really, really wanted Communion every week," was gratified by their decision, and the practice has become very important to Chuck. "The Communion becomes a natural flow as the Word tasted, seen, and shared," he reflected.

Relearning Church Planting

Just as NCDs tend to be different from established congregations, they are also different from each other, with differences linked to the local cultures, the character and demographics of their neighborhoods, and, of course, to the interests, skills, and priorities of early leaders. In the days when Presbyterian numbers were on the rise nationwide, NCDs were most commonly targeted for high-growth areas similar to the home bases of existing congregations. Nearly always, it was the presbytery that took the initiative to scout out likely prospects, conduct the necessary studies, create the budgets that supported an effort to organize a new congregation, and seek an organizing pastor. Established congregations were not usually reluctant to support the new projects, often even commissioning some of their own members to participate, because it seemed that there were plenty of potential Presbyterians to go around, and there was no need to feel threatened by the prospect of competing with a new congregation for members and funds. Today, strategies for developing new churches may follow the old models but frequently take new departures, particularly in considering start-ups in urban settings that might have been missed in earlier decades in the race to the suburbs. One example is the Upper Room Fellowship in Pittsburgh.

Several years ago, Pittsburgh Presbytery embarked on an effort to relearn how to do new church development. They set up a New Church Development Commission, and the Presbytery called Vera White, a former freelance writer and high school English and theater teacher, to serve on its staff as director of New Church Development, Stewardship, and the Committee on Ministry for Pittsburgh Presbytery. (Vera White is now associate for the Presbyterian Mission Agency's 1001 New Worshiping Communities project.) White has noted that "eighteen-to-thirty-year-olds are the most unchurched generation in the history of our nation. The traditional, institutional church as a whole has struggled to reach them."[4] When taking the

4. Website:http://www.onethousandone.org/News/1001-News/New-1001-Associate-Vera-White.aspx/.

position with the Mission Agency, White said that she also felt called to help Presbyterians reach out to new-immigrant groups and to inner-city African Americans.

In Pittsburgh, they came to believe that NCDs work best when not started from the top down, and several projects were initiated when the Presbytery affirmed calls that various persons in its midst were experiencing. Michael Gehrling and Christopher Brown felt a call to plant a new church, and consulted with Vera White. She encouraged Mike and Chris to take a "prayer walk"—a walk through a neighborhood that White thought might be the next logical step for an NCD. Gehrling and Brown followed her advice but did not feel a call to that neighborhood, and so sought out other urban neighborhoods for prayerful consideration, including one called Squirrel Hill. Squirrel Hill did not seem the likely target area for a Presbyterian NCD. It is largely Jewish, although 30 percent of the population is not involved with a worshiping community of any kind. Nevertheless, Gehrling and Brown felt that this might be the place for them. It is home to many graduate students, professors, and people with intellectual interests, a constituency that seemed to match the gifts and passions that Mike and Chris believed they brought to the project. Pittsburgh Presbytery heard their sense of call, affirmed it, and ordained them in 2008 specifically to organize a NCD in Squirrel Hill, then provided the structure and guidance necessary to move forward, setting goals and benchmarks, and providing funding for the start-up.

Both Gehrling and Brown are graduates of Pittsburgh Seminary. They had both participated in the seminary's World Mission Initiative, gaining experience with house churches in Southeast Asia that were growing in spite of limited resources and the use of methods that were not always traditional. The two are both half-time organizing pastors of the NCD, and each has another job. Brown is a barista, and Gehrling is a campus minister at Carnegie Mellon University with InterVarsity Christian Fellowship.

The Upper Room Fellowship began as a house church with eight people meeting in a living room, the coffee table serving as the Communion Table. Today, having outgrown the home setting, they meet in a rented storefront, and they hope to expand into part of an abandoned movie theater next door that is owned by the same landlord. Worship is at the classical hour of 11:00 a.m. on Sundays, and they have, from the very beginning, celebrated the Lord's Supper every week.

When asked what sort of demographic has been drawn to this NCD, Michael Gehrling replies, "Overwhelmingly, young adults." Most are professionals who are just starting out in various careers, or graduate students or young, tenure-track professors from the University of Pittsburgh or Carnegie Mellon University who are just beginning their academic careers. In addition, along with the younger generations, Upper Room counts a number of older, primarily single men from the same generation as the co-pastors' grandparents. In general, all these constituencies tend to be people who are thoughtful about their faith, reports Gehrling, and, although they are at different levels of maturity in understanding it, they are very intentional about taking the faith seriously.

The primary mode of contact with potential members is by word of mouth and by use of the Internet. Anyone looking for a church in Squirrel Hill can find them on the Net and read their mission statement, which includes these words: "We believe that God has called us to be a *cross-cultural, sacramental,* and *missional* community."[5] Gehrling agrees with the observations of others that younger generations are likely to be drawn to worship in ways that are expressive, through which they can feel themselves to be deeply engaged, and sacramental worship provides that. Working with a generation of young adults most of whom come from various Protestant backgrounds that are not noticeably, or at least consistently, sacramental, the co-pastors have been finding that the Eucharist is "highly, highly valued" by constituents who are delighted that it can be celebrated every week. It has become a way of discovering a deep connection with and among people.

Another tent-making NCD pastor is Jud Hendrix of Covenant Community Church in Louisville, Kentucky. The congregation was chartered in 2010, but the process of organizing began at least thirteen years earlier, after Jud and a colleague, Elizabeth Kaznak (who has since become full-time director of a nonprofit organization), had begun envisioning the project with their "launch team" two years before that. Jud and Liz, who had each been associate pastors in Presbyterian congregations in Louisville, were looking for another way of practicing Christian community around some different ecclesiological and theological models. To sum up their thought, they began using the word *postmodern.* The General Presbyter of Mid-Kentucky Presbytery, Betty Meadows, learned about their interest and suggested that they write up a church-development model. They studied some other projects,

---

5. http://www.pghupperroom.com/main/.

including the Church of the Savior in Washington DC, and devised their own version, which they understood to reflect Reformed and progressive traditions, and set as their target demographic the young-adult community in Louisville, particularly those who self-identified as "spiritual but not religious"—people who, for the most part, were not new to Christianity, but who had become "de-churched," finding Christianity and the church to be irrelevant for the most part.

As is often the case, the fledgling group began with worship in a home, but soon moved to a nesting place in the small, established James Lees Memorial Presbyterian Church in Louisville. While they did in fact attract persons who can be described as "spiritual but not religious," they also attracted some who were deeply committed to the church, but interested in doing church a new way. At one time, sixteen ordained ministers participated in the community. About a third of the worshipers are members of sexual minorities—lesbian, bisexual, gay, or transgendered—people whose experience had been to be disenfranchised by the church. Covenant Community does not identify as a More Light congregation, preferring to think of itself as post-orientation (i.e., feeling it unnecessary to adopt a specific designation to describe themselves in terms of one set of issues or another). Describing the interaction and interrelationships that have developed among the quite varied constituencies that meld in Covenant Community Church, Hendrix speaks of it as making for a "beautiful community."

When Covenant Community Presbyterian started, most of its members were from the targeted group, young adults, and the average age was twenty-seven or twenty-eight years old; but thirteen years have passed, and the average age is now older, and there are a lot of children. The congregation meets at 5:00 p.m. on Sundays, and they celebrate the Lord's Supper every week, with a meal following downstairs in the same building. Members of the community bring food to share, welcoming everyone with the expectation that not everyone will have brought a dish themselves. Occasionally they gather in smaller groups around tables in homes, with the intention of reclaiming coffee tables and lunch tables as examples of communion. Communal meals and their eucharistic worship are closely related.

From the beginning, Hendrix reports, they had been thinking about how to reembody worship, bringing the body and the senses back into their assembly, a purpose also expressed by some of the pastors who have introduced weekly celebration in established congregations. Hendrix describes the Lord's Supper as "a rich, tangible ritual . . . really important to us." Once they took a straw poll of the congregation, asking the hypothetical question whether, if, for the rest of their lives, members could either only hear a sermon or only receive communion, which would they choose? All but one person chose communion, which "is really the central piece of our community."

A Bridge Church

Back in Pittsburgh, where there have been eleven NCDs started over the past thirteen years (during the tenure of Vera White), you will want to make the acquaintance of the Hot Metal Bridge Faith Community. Yes, it really is called Hot Metal Bridge (HMB), the name drawn from a dream experienced by one of the co-pastors, Jim Walker, whose "waking dream" was of running with his friend, Jeff Eddings, across the Monongahela River on a span called the Hot Metal Bridge, which took its name from the era of steel production in Pittsburgh, when molten steel was transported across it to be poured into molds. Walker's dream was of Jesus calling to him from across the Hot Metal Bridge. Walker shared his dream with Eddings, with whom he is now co-pastor of the HMB Faith Community. Walker, a United Methodist minister, and Eddings, a minister of the PCUSA, launched a new faith community jointly sponsored by the two denominations.

Walker and Eddings, both graduates of Pittsburgh Seminary, had been doing youth ministry but could not miss the fact that the youth with whom they had worked went off to college never to be seen again. They imagined creating a bridge that would reach out to young adults, and they have experienced considerable success. The decision was made to place the church on the South Side, within a mile of eight different institutions of higher education. Walker and Eddings began by connecting with college students, and then, working through a local tattoo shop, they made connections with young adults in the countercultural scene—many musicians and artists—and they also made contact with homeless people, many of whom are also young adults. Of course, ten years have passed since making those first contacts, and a good many of those young adults who were drawn to the project early on have married, produced children, gotten jobs, and bought houses, so the profile of the congregation looks different now than it did then. In effect, the original mission has evolved into something else. HMB is less involved with outreach to students, but another nearby church plant has taken up that role. HMB has taken on a new life connecting with families with small children. Walker evaluates the change, saying,

> I think that's okay . . . I think that's just the way things are. When you start to build a community, it starts to take on a life of its own, and I think that's what has happened to us. That's how the church operates. And it's not a threat. The church is always supposed to be creating new communities of faith. It's part of the lifeblood of the church. We're supposed to worship, gather in community. And we should always be creating space for new people, and sometimes that means creating a whole new church for people to gather in.

Does that mean that HMB has become another conventional church? Not really. The Hot Metal Bridge Faith Community celebrates the Lord's Supper every week in both of its Sunday morning services. They decided to do that early on, knowing that their mission was directed to young adults; and young adults do not want to be a passive audience but to be actively involved in worship. The co-pastors understand the Sacrament as key to helping people apprehend that God is reaching out to establish communion with them all the time, not just when they gather on the Lord's Day. So, each service ends with Communion, immediately followed by some sort of meal. At the first service, it is a standing-up breakfast of bagels and coffee; at the second service, it is a sit-down meal. HMB also gathers for meals on Tuesday and Thursday nights. On those two nights, a bakery brings over their unsold bread and piles it on a table, and after dinner, people wrap up some bread to take home. HMB is clearly a community that understands its identity in terms of keeping the meal.

For about five years, the congregation met in a cafeteria they rented for worship. The landlord terminated the relationship, and the community found itself literally homeless. For a while they met under a bridge on the South Side, and then found an old garage to meet in. After that, the United Methodist bishop helped them purchase a bar that HMB renovated. (A video posted on their website shows a number of former churches in the neighborhood that have become bars, restaurants, or homes—and a vacant lot where once stood a United Methodist Church. HMB is the solitary example of a reverse transformation—a bar becoming a church!) The renovated space in the former bar will accommodate about two hundred people for worship, and both of their Sunday services are pretty well filled. They have no plans to add other services.

When they renovated the bar, the architect conceived the idea of hanging on the walls the tables needed for meals. The wall-mounted tables unfold when they are needed. Two artists in the church have painted murals on the tables. On one wall, a series of murals on the tabletops depicts bread being made: soil tilled, seeds planted, wheat growing, grain harvested, dough being kneaded, bread being broken. On the other wall the murals are similar, but represent the fruit of the vine, from growing in the vineyard to being poured. Again in this worshiping community it is doubly evident that meal keeping is central to its sense of identity.

Walker describes the Eucharist as he has experienced it in a way that is similar to what Elizabeth Deibert or James Lee seem to be saying when they use the word *mystery*.

> I think there is a supernatural quality about sharing in the Lord's Supper each week. There's something powerful about it. I can't prove it, but I think something happens. The Holy Spirit does move, and I've witnessed some really cool things over the years as we've done this week after week after week, and when you stand in line with a kid with a blue Mohawk and covered with blue tattoos, and behind you is a homeless person who's hung over and you share this meal with all these people, it just turns your world upside down.

Walker describes people who might be serving the communicants as "some of the most broken people you ever laid eyes on holding the bread and the cup . . . people who are just hungry and broken and lonely and hurting, and here they are holding the cup . . . It's transformational, impactful . . ."

What Motivates Trailblazers?

In most congregations, whether long established or brand new, pastors are going to have a key role in the shaping of Sacramental practice. The easier thing, when becoming pastor of an existing congregation, is to learn its culture and adjust to whatever practices are already in place. After all, there is a chance that change might be resisted rather than affirmed or consented to, and normally there are issues aplenty demanding the attention of the pastor and church officers; so what motivates a pastor to initiate a more central role for Holy Communion in the weekly worshiping assembly? Later chapters will look more closely at the dynamics of decision making in congregations, but what if we could ask some of these pastors and organizing pastors in weekly-Eucharist churches what made this issue so important to them that they were willing to stick their necks out?

Moderator Neal Presa, pastor of the Middlesex Presbyterian Church, had become active in denominational life and had served on the General Assembly Council. Like many of his ministerial colleagues, he was not uninterested in the Sacraments, but his attention and commitments had been focused in other directions. In 2003–2004, Presa was invited to serve on the General Assembly's Sacraments Study Group that was formed to reflect on and respond to an overture to the 1998 General Assembly from Central Washington Presbytery asking for guidance with respect to Sacramental practice, and specifically, with respect to the relationship between Baptism and Eucharist. (It was the Study Group that ultimately produced *Invitation to Christ*.[6])

As Neal took part in the deliberations of the Study Group, he became more and more engaged with the issues they were examining, and when he came back home to Middlesex after meetings, he shared his discoveries with the elders of the church, and they could see that he was energized by the things he was learning. The Moderator testifies that it was participating in this task force that redirected his interests to the point that he felt led to make a sharp turn in his doctoral program. He already had a ThM in pastoral theology from Princeton Seminary in addition to his MDiv from San Francisco Seminary. After moving to Middlesex, he had begun a PhD program at Drew University in Psychology and Religion, and had already completed a semester in that program. Neal's experience with the Study Group caused him to make a move that was unprecedented at Drew, and that was to ask to change from one doctoral program to another—from Psychology and Religion to the program in Liturgy. In order to make the switch and keep up with his new cohort in liturgical studies, he had to immerse himself in learning what they had already had a semester to absorb. Neal Presa testifies that the Holy Spirit used these two experiences—the work of the task force and his academic studies—to help him see that when it came to the church's sacramental life, "there was more than meets the eye here."

How did Vice Moderator Tom Trinidad find himself as a pastor strongly advocating weekly Communion? Trinidad came to the Christian faith through Young Life and helped to organize Wyldlife, a version of Young Life for Junior High students. He became a Presbyterian while

---

6. Presbyterian Church (USA), *Invitation*.

interning in music and youth at First Presbyterian Church in Colorado Springs. He reports having had no special appetite for weekly Eucharist until he studied John Calvin and his sacramental theology, and Calvin's desire for the sacrament to accompany and seal the Word. In a worship class at Princeton Seminary, he remembers encountering a book by Hughes Oliphant Old in which, as Trinidad remembers it, Old declared that "covenant theology is Reformed sacramental theology." This intrigued him, and he wanted to explore that further.

After seminary, Trinidad became chaplain of Central College in Pella, Iowa, an institution of the Reformed Church in America. Pella, a town with a population of ten thousand, not only had Lutheran, Methodist, Baptist, Roman Catholic, Orthodox, and nondenominational churches, but it also had thirteen churches with some sort of Reformed identity (though no Presbyterian church). In this milieu, Trinidad determined that he "wanted to be a voice of invitation to greater ecumenical relationships, and that the Sacraments would be a primary way to do that." The Vice Moderator was drawn to Notre Dame's doctoral program in liturgics because James White, the late Methodist liturgical historian and theologian, was teaching there at the time, and Trinidad had read White's books. He discovered a confessionally diverse community of teachers and colleagues at Notre Dame that exposed him to a deep study of sacramental theology from an ecumenical perspective. His studies led him to a desire to reintroduce among Presbyterians a more Calvinian rather than Zwinglian appreciation of the Lord's Supper, understanding the Sacraments as deeply important in the formation of Christian discipleship. Tom felt some resonance with the early Barth, who wrote in *The Preaching of the Gospel*: "There is indeed no preaching, in the precise meaning of the term, except when it is accompanied and illuminated by the sacrament . . . And this is precisely what we lack today: the sacrament every Sunday."[7]

Like Presa, Trinidad had served on the General Assembly's Sacraments Study Group. He became the designated pastor at Faith Presbyterian Church in Colorado Springs, then the called pastor in 2010. Before he was chosen to be designated pastor, he told the committee that interviewed him, "If you call me to this church, I'm from the first Sunday going to be talking about the importance of Communion, and keep it up until we have weekly Communion." Some were shocked, and others intrigued, but his honesty and his directness apparently appealed to them.

---

7. Barth, *Preaching*, 23, 25.

Come and See

Chip Andrus was raised in a Southern Baptist church until he was twelve years old, although his grandfather was a Presbyterian minister, and he is descended from a line of Presbyterian ministers that reaches all the way back to Scotland—the first of them having come to America in about 1640. He marks his commitment to weekly Eucharist as stemming from his experience as a student at Louisville Presbyterian Seminary, where they celebrated the Sacrament every week in chapel. Andrus became absorbed in reading about and studying worship, naming particularly books by James White, and one by Alexander Schmemann called *Introduction to Liturgical Theology*.[8] Chip was reflecting on these things and became convinced that this was the rhythm the church should be following: a primary rhythm of Word and Sacrament as a weekly celebration. Andrus believes that the formative power of the liturgy is such that it shapes both a sense of Christ's "real presence" and an ethical imperative. He was outspoken enough in his conviction that some of his fellow students at Louisville Seminary began to tease him by calling him "the weekly-Eucharist guy."

Chip led the church in Harrison, Arkansas, to weekly Communion, and now, as pastor of the South Salem Presbyterian Church in New York, he has done the same there. Andrus understands the meal "through the resurrection to be a supper with the crucified and risen one—not a meal in the shadow of the cross as would be a 'Last Supper.'" Andrus was encouraged by the example of Fred Anderson.

Anderson, who first introduced weekly Communion to the Pine Street Church in Harrisburg, then at Madison Avenue in New York City, traces his motivation to the liturgical studies underway at Princeton Seminary during the 1970s, particularly the influence of Professors Edward Dowey and Arlo Duba, as well as to the teaching of Princeton University scholars such as Professor Horton Davies. From them he learned both of Calvin's high sacramental theology and of the Reformer's desire for worship that included both preaching and the Lord's Supper every week. Anderson served on the task force that developed the current *Directory for Worship*, approved by the General Assembly in 1989, and he was among several who brought to their work a passion for weekly Eucharist. It was during the time of his service on the task force that he decided that he would attempt to introduce the practice at Pine Street.

At some point in his active ministry, David Batchelder, now serving West Plano Church, began to feel a certain restlessness with the typical

---

8. Schmemann, *Introduction*.

Sunday morning practice with which he was familiar—a restlessness stemming both from intellectual questions and his personal experience as a pastor and as a father. The intellectual exploration began with an awareness that Word, Sacrament, and Sunday are all intimately related, creating an energy in him for digging deeper into the historical, biblical, and theological roots of that relationship, which he was able to do when he began working on a Doctor of Ministry degree at Austin Seminary. As a pastor and a father, his experience paralleled that of many others who become concerned about passing on the faith to their own children and to the children of the congregation. Christian educators have created various devices to put in the hands of children to be used during a service (pictures and fill-in-the-blank worksheets) to help them notice aspects of the environment, the liturgy, the readings, and the sermon; but even that seems to highlight how word oriented Presbyterian worship tends to be. As Batchelder pursued his DMin in Worship and Liturgy, he felt himself moved to a growing appreciation for symbol and ritual and the power of material signs to manifest that which they represent. In short, he felt himself converted to a deep conviction of incarnational theology, and along with it, to a sacramental vision of liturgy and life. What he learned, he tested in experience, and found it to be beautiful and true, as well as deeply satisfying.

Sid Burgess, pastor at Edgewood Church in Birmingham, Alabama, credits his commitment to weekly Communion with his chapel experience at Columbia Seminary, where they celebrated the Sacrament every Friday. He also had the benefit of practical role models in the persons of Rick and Elizabeth Deibert, also Columbia Seminary graduates, who were the organizing pastors of Immanuel Church in Montgomery, Alabama (in the same presbytery as Edgewood), which has been celebrating the Sacrament weekly from the beginning. Sid was raised a Southern Baptist (in a denomination that prefers the word *ordinance* to *sacrament*), and he has followed a path not unfamiliar to others who have become Presbyterians while on an adult faith journey. When embracing the Reformed tradition is a decision carefully considered and intentional, it often leads those new to Presbyterianism to try to learn how to be Presbyterians by paying respectful attention to the details in the *Book of Order*, including the *Directory for Worship*, as well as to the root theology that one finds in exploring Calvin, the Reformer who was the primary actor in defining the Reformed/Presbyterian tradition. It was, perhaps, such a journey that led Burgess to embrace and become an advocate for the Service for the Lord's Day, for which the norm is weekly Communion.

Come and See

Elizabeth Deibert's experience at Immanuel Church in Montgomery deepened her commitment to weekly celebration of the Sacrament and led her to a resolve to institute the practice at Peace Church in Lakewood Ranch. She advocated weekly Communion from the very beginning, and reassured those who had reservations about it, saying, "If you try this for six months, I guarantee that you will not want to go back," and that has indeed proved to be the case.

James Lee, the pastor at New Covenant Fellowship in Austin, when asked why the congregation had come to practice weekly Communion, simply replied that "It was something we discerned in the very beginning . . . What was important was that the Lord's Supper was a celebration. It felt like what we needed, and became part of what we are as a church." Covenant Church, in Austin, from whom the initiative came to form a multicultural congregation, celebrates the meal weekly in one of its services, and while there is no record of a direct influence from Covenant to New Covenant, a number of people from Covenant were part of the original group, and it was a natural part of the culture with which they had been acquainted there.

In the case of the Mendenhalls, Laura had been a believer in and advocate for weekly Eucharist for some time. Laura is one more person who had been influenced by the late Professor Stan Hall from Austin Seminary, who had been a friend when she was pastor at Westminster Church in the Texas capital. On the other hand, Chuck Mendenhall reflects that "after discovering the experience [of weekly Communion], I began to think about it theologically, but it was the doing of it every week that began to filter down into my psyche." For many, as for Chuck Mendenhall, conviction follows practice—with experience rather than intellectual commitment taking the lead.

In the case of co-pastors Michael Gehrling and Chris Brown at the Upper Room NCD in Pittsburgh, both had come to the conviction that weekly Eucharist was the ideal for the church, a conviction that had been kindled by their seminary coursework. They cite, for example, their studies with John Burgess, professor of systematic theology at Pittsburgh Seminary. Pursuing the ideal particularly commended itself as they considered the cultural environment of Squirrel Hill, the neighborhood where they felt called to base their work. The fact that it was a predominantly Jewish neighborhood meant that the celebration of Jewish festivals was both public and visible, and this "sacramental" aspect of Jewish faith—embodied not just in ideas but in rites—made worship practiced in a sacramental way a reasonable way of finding a complementary Christian identity for Upper Room in largely Jewish Squirrel Hill.

Jud Hendrix of Covenant Community Church in Louisville recalled that early on, he and his colleague had not intended that worship would be a particularly identifying characteristic of the NCD. Their concern was with developing Christian community after the manner of intentional communities. And yet somehow the organizing pastors simply assumed weekly Communion. They had always found the Table to be central and powerful in their own experience. "I don't know that we even questioned it," Hendrix muses. "It was just very important that we do Communion every week."

The Hot Metal Bridge Faith Community in Pittsburgh framed a mission statement that involved starting a church that would be a bridge to Jesus Christ. How? By helping people participate in the kingdom of God, defined as participating in "communion, community, compassion, and the proclamation of the word of God."[9] Each called for a specific strategy. To form a sense of communion, according to Jim Walker, there must be a means of grace to help us connect an outward sign with an inward grace. "We're already sharing in communion with God. The Lord's Supper is an outward sign of that. It's a celebration of what's already happening. And we decided it is kind of key to have Communion every week if we want to help people participate in communion with God." Walker, one of the co-pastors, affirms that the experience of the community has validated their original intuition that weekly Eucharist was the way to shape their congregation. His reading of the congregation's experience is that going to the Table is an outward expression of communion with God that is "far more powerful than anything done prior to that moment in the worship service."

As pastors reflect on factors that motivated them to try to introduce the practice of weekly Communion either in an established congregation or in a new church development, it becomes clear that the motivation seems to emerge from one of two sources: either from study, or from experience or observation, and sometimes the two together.

---

9. Since I copied the original quotation from the mission statement, it appears to have been reworded on their website. It is now: "We will be a bridge to Jesus Christ by participating in communion, welcoming all into community, listening and having compassion, growing in our faith and sharing Christ's story with the community of the South Side, the surrounding neighborhoods, and the world." http://www.hotmetalbridge.com/p/who-we-are.html/.

"My Eyes Were Opened"

Brant Copeland, pastor of First Presbyterian Church in Tallahassee, has described what he feels strongly enough to call a kind of conversion experience. "Like countless Christians before me," he writes, "I have come to experience the risen Christ 'in the breaking of the bread' . . . For me. . . recognizing the risen Christ at his Table came only after years of failure to recognize him there."[10]

Copeland grew up a child of the manse in the former Southern Presbyterian Church, where he was not admitted to the Lord's Table until the age of twelve, like most American Presbyterians of his generation. He made his first profession of faith at a Maundy Thursday service and there received communion for the first time. As Copeland describes the Communion services of his childhood, they were infrequent and solemn, somber and reverent. Citing the late James White, Copeland quotes White's assessment of the Lord's Supper after the Enlightenment as basically a "mixture of Enlightenment morality and Zwinglian theology." "The essence of thousands of communion sermons continues to be: 'Jesus died; Be good.' This is certainly the predominant view in much of American Protestantism (and at the popular level probably much of Roman Catholicism.) And it is perfectly in accord with the Enlightenment tenet that religion's chief purpose is to be morally edifying."[11]

After Copeland graduated from Southwestern at Memphis (now Rhodes College), he matriculated in the University of St. Andrews in Scotland, where he began the academic study of theology. The University Chapel is at the heart of Brant's "conversion experience." There they celebrated the Lord's Supper every Lord's Day, with either the (Presbyterian) Church of Scotland chaplain or the Anglican chaplain presiding.

"There, in the shadow of John Knox's own pulpit, we shared the bread and cup of the risen Christ. It is perhaps too dramatic to say, 'My eyes were opened, and I recognized him,' but I can think of no more accurate way to say it. This was no mere memorial meal . . . it was without a doubt a celebration!"[12]

Many of the words were the same words Copeland had been accustomed to at Communion services back home, but "the ethos was entirely

---

10. Copeland, *Eucharist*, 4.
11. White, *Brief History*, 155.
12. Copeland, *Eucharist*, 6.

different. This was not a recapitulation of the Last Supper. It was a celebration of the presence of the risen Christ." For Brant Copeland, these eucharistic celebrations provided a new lens through which to view his life, his place in the church of Jesus Christ, and his emerging vocation as a minister of the Word and Sacraments. In his case, as in many others, it was a particular kind of sacramental experience that came first, then years of study that shed light on the experience and helped to bring it to maturity. Copeland has devoted years of his ministry to sharing with his congregation what he has discovered: in the sacramental meal, we meet the risen Christ; and this meal is rightly celebrated every Lord's Day.

Two

Will It Bring the Numbers Up?

The elder's question was an earnest one. After a workshop on Sacraments offered by his presbytery, he approached the presenter who had advocated weekly Communion, and asked, "If we do what you say, will it bring back the numbers we had in the 1950s?" One could almost hear the desperation in his voice. If there were anything to be done to reverse the declining numbers, he would be willing to consider it whether it made sense to him or not.

He is not alone. Not only those who vividly remember the full churches of the 1950s but also many for whom that era is only a rumor, including their pastors, sometimes feel desperate to discover some program, some recipe, some technology or strategy that will lead to a return of the days of full sanctuaries, climbing memberships, and overflowing treasuries. Unfortunately, even if there were such a remedy, desperation rarely serves us well and can cause us to race each other in the wrong direction.

Since the parking lots of the megachurches that have sprung up within recent memory are still full, and some of the young families that visit our church end up joining one of those, we fail to notice that their numbers, generally speaking, are beginning to decline too. Even the Southern Baptist Convention, which is so focused on growth and does not have a reputation for strenuous record keeping, is seeing the numbers go down. So, even those recently fast-growing churches built to be architecturally appealing to baby boomers who reported a distaste for churchiness—even the competition across town that can afford to acquire and program the most advanced technology in-house, the churches that never owned an organ and have carefully attuned their worship to a sophisticated understanding of generational nuance—even they are not immune from the larger social forces that have led to declining church membership.

The short answer to the elder's earnest question is, No, weekly Communion will not bring back the 1950s. Nor will better preaching, world music, attractive and accessible spaces, great nurseries, abundant restrooms, or plenty of parking. However useful those things may be, they will not restore the cultural moment that was the unique product of that postwar era in which Americans united to raise the banners of faith so as to define our society as godly in contrast to godless Communism.

A good case can be made for restoring the Sacraments to their rightful place in the active practice of Christian faith, but the case does not rest on a claim that rediscovering the essential unity of Word and Sacrament will reverse the tides of history and restore mainstream Christianity to its former place of dominance. Nevertheless, if Presbyterians want to do their part in reaching out to the alienated and the indifferent, they will do well to take into account that the whole of Western culture has crossed an enormous historical frontier, moving several steps beyond the pervasive Enlightenment model for engaging with the world. "New occasions teach new duties," as the James Russell Lowell poem says.

Educators, including those involved in Christian education, have already noticed this, and have understood that having crossed that boundary calls for greater diversity in educational strategies. In this post-Enlightenment culture, it is quite clear that people interact with their environment, with other people, and with all things visible and invisible not only with the conscious mind but with the whole self, including with all the senses. Emerging generations are those most likely to have both feet planted in the developing post-Enlightenment era, while ways of worship that were adapted to the earlier era are less and less effective in engaging them. Fred Anderson, pastor at Madison Avenue, has welcomed a number of refugees from a church with a reputation for using the Enlightenment model (didacticism) very effectively, but who have tired of worship that relies almost exclusively on absorbing information via the ear and the word-processing mind. Nor is it any solution to try to involve people in worship by having them read large quantities of print out loud, a familiar Presbyterian strategy. In our society we are overwhelmed by the sheer quantity of both words and images, and while both can be vessels of the holy, the fact that in our society they can and are frequently used to manipulate requires not only that the church use them with scrupulous care, but that they be accompanied and even interpreted by nonverbal and tangible means of celebrating the gospel.

Holistic engagement requires something more than we have been accustomed to, and Elizabeth Deibert and James Lee rightly use the deliberately imprecise word *mystery* to point us in the right direction. *Mystery* is a biblical word (e.g., Rom 16:25, Eph 1:9), and it leads us to something much more profound than a riddle to be solved. As Calvin said, "Nothing remains but to break forth in wonder at this mystery, which plainly neither the mind is able to conceive nor the tongue to express."[1] We encounter the holy as whole persons, bringing our intuition, our hunches, our hunger and thirst, our relationships, our history both bodily and spiritual as well as our questions and our reflecting, thinking, pondering intellects trying to sort it all out. When it comes to the Sacraments, including the Sacramental meal, there's more to it than meets the eye, as Moderator Presa has put it; or as Jim Walker of Hot Metal Bridge Faith Community has said, "I can't prove it, but I think something happens."

God Provides

As desperate as we may feel when ways the church used to engage the holy God for generations seem inadequate on their own to meet the spiritual needs of new generations in a new era, it is not necessary to wait for the next bigger-than-life pastoral personality to invent a heretofore unimagined way ahead. Nor is it necessary for all of us to become Pentecostals, whose worship may engage the body as well as the spirit, but not in a way that is likely to appeal to everyone. Providentially, historic churches like the PCUSA are not without resources of our own. Even if not employed to the fullest, our church already has in its spiritual repertoire Baptism and Eucharist, God's own gifts, along with preaching, for the spiritual nourishment and strengthening of the people of God. Having these gifts, it is both our duty and our delight to use them as faithfully as we can.

The church of Jesus Christ is doctrinal, but Christian faith is not only about doctrine. Christianity is a way of believing, of perceiving reality, but also of experiencing and tasting that reality, and not just of hearing about it or thinking about it. It is about conviction, but the conviction is rooted and nourished in concrete practices. Much as we value doctrine, when the church reads its Bible not merely as a manual of doctrine, it is likely to

1. Calvin, *Institutes* 4.17.7, 1367.

discover that both Christianity and Judaism are, each in its own way, meal-keeping movements.

The Old Testament testifies that Jethro, Aaron, and all the elders of Israel gathered to eat bread together in celebration of delivery from the Egyptians, and they ate "in the presence of God" (Exod 18:1, 9–12). When Israel had received God's law on Sinai and pledged to keep it, Moses and Aaron and seventy elders of Israel "beheld God, and they ate and drank" (Exod 24:3–11). (Brevard Childs, the late Old Testament scholar, a Presbyterian himself, describes this meal as a "eucharistic festival."[2]) In a passage from Deuteronomy that exhorts the people to worship in a central place of God's choosing, God commands the people to bring their offerings and tithes and "eat there in the presence of the Lord your God, you and your households together, rejoicing" (Deut 12:1–7). Note the twin emphases in which these meals are characterized by God's "presence" and by "rejoicing," characteristics equally descriptive of the church's experience with the Lord's Supper.

Of course, the Passover meal is a prime example of Jewish meal keeping. The three Synoptic Gospels (Matthew, Mark, and Luke) describe Jesus's last supper with his disciples as a Passover meal, and although John does not, he places it within the orbit of the Passover festival. In the Passover meal, various foods symbolically represent aspects of the exodus from Egypt. For example, bitter herbs represent the bitterness of the people's bondage in Egypt, and unleavened bread is a reminder that they had to flee in haste. Part of the responsibility of the host who presides at the Passover meal is to interpret the details of the meal, including the symbolic role of the foods. In the case of Jesus's last supper with his disciples, the Synoptics identify Jesus as having taken the role of presider, but in this case he lifted up not the bitter herbs but the bread and cup, interpreting them as symbols of himself, his flesh and blood, his very being.

Jewish ways of keeping meals as before God are not just curious details of an old regime, but they lie at the root of Jesus's own meal keeping, and the church's. It is no accident that all four Gospels include stories of the feeding of the multitudes, nor is it a coincidence that they use the same sequence of verbs to describe those meals as was used to describe the actions of the last supper: taking, blessing, breaking, and giving. The New Testament names other meals as well, including meals eaten with sinners,

---

2. Childs, *Book of Exodus*, 507.

postresurrection meals, and eschatological meals—all of which played a role in the shaping of the Christian Eucharist.

Critiquing Practice in New Testament Times

We Presbyterians are part of a deep tradition that takes the Bible very seriously, but we are not above the need to critique the practices we have received. We cherish as part of our definition of who we are the old slogan that identifies us as an *ecclesia reformata, semper reformanda secundum verbi dei* ("a reformed church, always being reformed according to the word of God"). The last phrase, *secundum verbi dei* ("according to the word of God"), has too often been omitted when we recite it. In any given generation, we may be biblical but not always as biblical as we might be, or ought to be.

Gordon Lathrop has argued that a purpose of each of the four Gospels was to reform practices in the various Christian congregations based on the writer's perception of deficiencies in practice. A primary concern, continuing what the Apostle Paul had begun in 1 Corinthians and Galatians, was to critique and reform the churches' meal practices. In the letter to the church at Corinth, Paul had criticized meal practices in which there was a lack of respect for the dignity of some members of the church. In Galatians, he criticized Peter for his willingness to see two separate tables in the church in Antioch, if necessary, to satisfy those who were squeamish about Jewish Christians sharing the same table as Gentile Christians. The four Evangelists, following the example of Paul, did not believe that reform was something to be undertaken only once and then forgotten.

> The diverse but converging reform interests of the New Testament Gospels show that the assemblies for which they were originally intended were complex communities, with differing challenges. They were made up of people who belonged to their age and were, in diverse ways, both trying to belong and trying to distinguish themselves from others. They were sorting out the meanings of their Christian faith, sometimes brilliantly, sometimes not. The Gospel books intended to help them with this sorting. And the Gospel books intended especially to help them understand the purpose and the practice of their assemblies.[3]

---

3. Lathrop, *Four Gospels*, 148.

One of many examples of a Gospel's critique of then-current meal practices in the New Testament era is found in Luke 14, in which Jesus contrasts the culture of people competing for status with another way, the way of the kingdom (reign) of God, saying, "But when you are invited, go and sit down at the lowest place" (Luke 14:10). One might make the case that, in every generation, the church is always made up of "complex communities," of people who belong to their age, trying to sort out the meanings of their Christian faith, "sometimes brilliantly, sometimes not." To put it another way, the church will always be in need of "being reformed according to the word of God."

Among the four Gospels, Luke most consistently highlights meals, including what may rightly be described as the first *Lord's* Supper (in contrast with *Last* Supper). The first Lord's Supper occurs in the story of the road to Emmaus, in which the risen Lord appears to two disciples on the first Easter afternoon. They do not recognize him. When they arrive at their destination after his perambulating interpretation of Scripture, he consents to join them for the evening meal. "When he was at the table with them, he *took* bread, *blessed* and *broke* it, and *gave* it to them." (Note the telltale eucharistic sequence of these four verbs.) Luke continues, "Then their eyes were opened and they recognized him" (Luke 24:10–11). Lathrop argues that the Emmaus narrative is a paradigm for the gatherings of the Christian assemblies. We are meant to encounter the crucified and risen Christ in two ways that are both apparent in the narrative: in the Scriptures and their interpretation in the meeting, and also in the bread taken, blessed, broken, and given. The two belong together and neither should be neglected.

Similarly, the Gospel of John concludes with two Sunday gatherings in a closed room: the first when the Apostle Thomas is absent, the second when he is present (John 21:19–29). The two Sunday gatherings in which the risen Lord becomes present to the disciples foreshadow "the continuation of Sunday in the life of the Christian movement."[4] It is clear from 1 Cor 11:23–26, one of the earliest New Testament writings, that at least by the early fifties of the first century the churches were celebrating the Lord's Supper. Certainly by the time that Luke had written Acts (around 85–95 CE), it had become established practice that the meal was a part of the assembly for worship on the Lord's Day, "the first day of the week" (Acts 20:7). Rooted in Jesus's own ministry, meal keeping became an identifying feature of early Christian communal life: "They devoted themselves to the

---

4. Ibid., 135.

apostles teaching and fellowship, to the breaking of bread and the prayers" (Acts 2:42).

In the mid-second century, according to Justin Martyr, the practice in Rome, where he was writing, was for the church to gather "on the day which is called Sunday." They read Scripture, preached, prayed, and then proceeded to offer thanksgiving over the elements, which then were "distributed and received by each one; and they are sent to the absent by the deacons."[5]

From its beginning, the church was a meal-keeping movement that grew out of and was profoundly influenced by the Jewish community and its meal-keeping practices. The church's practices were subjected to reforming critiques that are embedded in the New Testament from the earlier writings to the later. So, while it is imperative that the church today become consciously and intentionally aware of the major cultural changes that we are all experiencing as we transition to a new historical era that both values and yet moves beyond the four centuries of Enlightenment dominance, that this experience of transition is not the only reason for rediscovering our sacramental roots. Yes, we need to adapt to a new cultural paradigm that includes the body as well as the spirit, just as we adapted so well to the Enlightenment paradigm in which we presumed that there is nothing that is not explainable and cannot be put into words in a purely logical argument. We have entered a new era, yes, and we would be wise to adapt to it, but there is another imperative at least as pressing: the need to be faithful in using everything that God has given the church to sustain it for its mission in every generation. "Put on the whole armor of God" (Eph 6:11).

Critiquing Practice in the Reformation and Beyond

The need to critique eucharistic practice did not end with the New Testament. In early centuries, not only was every Lord's Day service one of both Word and Eucharist, but the practice was for the congregation as a whole to participate in communion. However, by the medieval period prior to the Reformation, even though the Mass was celebrated every week, the people had become less and less inclined actually to commune, in part because the piety of the time had so stressed "the *tremendous distance* that separates us from God," and that piety had gained "greater and greater power over the

---

5. Justin Martyr, *First Apology*, 67, in Thompson, *Liturgies*, 9.

Christian mind."[6] The faithful scarcely dared to approach the altar. Added to that was the requirement that those who wished to commune first had to make penitential confession to a priest and receive absolution. "In addition, various cases of exclusion from the Sacrament were established in the spirit of the Old Testament purification laws, especially for married people and women . . . Greater and greater requirements were set down for the preparation. A synod of Coventry in 1237 desired a previous fast of half a week for lay people."[7] As a result, faithful people typically abstained from communing, although they were eager to watch the action of the priest at the altar, and sometimes even raced from one parish church to another, hoping to arrive in time to hear the Sanctus Bell signal that the miracle of transubstantiation had taken place so that they could "commune with the eyes" as the priest elevated the host.

The Synod of Agde (506 CE) in Gaul had already insisted that the faithful must receive communion three times a year at least: on Christmas, Easter, and Pentecost. By 1215, it had become necessary for the Lateran Council to require communion once a year, at Easter, as the new minimum. Official actions taken by the church in council were intended to challenge the practice of infrequent communion that had become the norm even though Mass was celebrated at least every Sunday.

Of course, the Protestant Reformation provides a sterling example of the critique of established sacramental practice. Not only did the Reformers challenge official sacramental theology, but they criticized actual practice, which inevitably embodied and sustained a theology of both the official and the unofficial sort. For the Reformers, it was first of all necessary that the Lord's Supper be a communal act for the whole congregation rather than the work of the priests alone or a devotional act of individual piety for what few of the people might dare to approach the Table. For both Martin Luther and John Calvin, there was no doubt that the Supper was to accompany the word every Lord's Day, as they understood that it had done as early as New Testament times and for generations following.

Luther's conviction was realized for a century or two, but weekly Communion in Lutheran congregations gradually dried up by the eighteenth century, when the Enlightenment was in full bloom. Calvin was less successful in his reform of the Eucharist than Luther. Critical of communing only once a year, as was common in the medieval church, Calvin said that

6. Jungmann, *Mass*, 500.
7. Ibid., 499.

"it should have been done far differently: the Lord's Table should have been spread at least once a week for the assembly of Christians."[8] Citing the book of Acts, he also said, "Thus it became the unvarying rule that no meeting of the church should take place without the Word, prayers, partaking of the Supper, and almsgiving."[9]

Calvin had gone to Geneva in the first place in response to an appeal by one of his reforming predecessors there (Guillaume Farel), and when he arrived, the practice of Communion three times a year was already in place. Farel had been influenced by Zwingli, the Reformer of Zurich, in whose view the Lord's Supper was understood to be, to put it too simply, a memorial meal in commemoration of a past event. It is well known that the city council of Geneva, who had ecclesiastical as well as civil power, overruled Calvin's earnest desire—to see Christian worship restored to its biblical roots of (a) Scripture and sermon, plus (b) the Lord's Supper every week—probably for reasons that were practical rather than consciously theological.

Calvin's Plan B was to rotate the Lord's Supper in the several parish churches of Geneva, so that at least one of them was celebrating the meal every week, preferably in someplace that would be convenient for and could accommodate most of the faithful, but he was not successful in that plan either. Ultimately, Genevan practice came to be Communion four times a year: at Christmas, Easter, Pentecost, and honoring a patron saint of the city, in September. It was a compromise, to put the best face on it, and it did mean that whole congregations celebrated the feast communally, but it fell short of what the Reformer wanted, and Calvin did not mince words. He called it a "defect" not to worship in both Word and Sacrament every Lord's Day. Calvin's successors did not manage to heal the defective practice, which, over time, acquired the sanctity that tradition may provide, whether for good or ill. The rationalistic influence of the Enlightenment that affected Lutheran eucharistic practice influenced the Reformed as well, cementing in place a form of worship that privileged the Word at the expense of the Sacrament. In Britain, hard-line Puritanism combined with the rationalism of the era to form a symbiotic relationship that combined, at least in the popular mind, to exalt words and scorn ritual action.

---

8. Calvin, *Institutes* 4.17.46, 1424.

9. Ibid., 4.17.44, 1422.

"Being Reformed"—Again

However, even when it seems as though no one will ever challenge a status quo, the Spirit still moves, and like it or not, the church discovers itself "being reformed" as the slogan goes, once again. By the last third of the nineteenth century, a few Presbyterians in both Scotland and the United States had begun to rediscover Calvin, and particularly to rediscover his sacramental theology and liturgical intentions. Some of them published English translations of the service books created by Calvin and by John Knox, the Scottish Reformer, which had been among the first ever to be placed in the hands of Christian congregations of any confession. Eventually, one of the fruits of their scholarship was to be, in the United States, the first *Book of Common Worship*, published in 1906. Contemporary practice had been subjected to a critique rooted in deeper acquaintance with Reformed origins.

The twentieth century witnessed several movements that had begun in the previous century and that gave momentum to the process of review and critique not only among Presbyterians and Reformed, but among other Protestants, and among Roman Catholics as well, both in Europe and North America. In the twentieth century, a revival of interest in biblical scholarship led to new insights about Scripture itself. If one reads Scripture looking only for history, doctrine, or ethics, that is what one is likely to find, but if one is open to other discoveries, it becomes possible to see things, for example, that illumine the roots of Baptism and the meal, and that help to unfold their richly layered meanings. The biblical theology movement fed into critiques of present practice on many levels, and it was accompanied by a rising interest in historical studies, including the study of Christian worship and its development. The twentieth-century ecumenical movement not only made use of all the emerging scholarship but also resulted in conversation and dialogue across confessional lines, which contributed to self-examination in all the historic denominations and confessional bodies.

In the 1960s, this flowering of attention to things biblical, historical, and liturgical led Roman Catholics, in Vatican Council II, to carry out a revolutionary critique of the liturgical practice that had been in place since the Counter-Reformation. Resulting changes in the Mass must have been experienced by most Catholics as an ecclesiastical earthquake. In fact, the post-Vatican II Mass resembles Calvin's ideal more than it resembles pre-Vatican II Catholic practice. Scripture is read from both Testaments, priests are encouraged to preach, and Communion is intended for the whole community. Communion is normally received in both bread and cup; communicants stand rather than kneel at an altar rail, just as, standing, the congregation had received the Supper at the Communion Table in Calvin's Geneva.

In the same decade of the 1960s, the former Northern Presbyterian Church, in 1961, and the Southern church, in 1963, each revised their *Directories for Worship*, the first major revisions since 1788. Robert McAfee Brown, whose own life and work was influenced by both Karl Barth and Reinhold Niebuhr, was responsible for drafting the revised *Directory* for the United Presbyterian Church in the U.S.A. Brown was known for having authored a popular book on the Bible that was used as part of the renowned Faith and Life Curriculum, as well as for his commitment to both scholarship and social justice. The revised *Directory* lifted up joy in the resurrection as the focus of Christian worship, and stated that "it is fitting that [the Lord's Supper] be observed as frequently as on each Lord's Day."[10]

With the new *Directory* laying the groundwork, drafts of the Service for the Lord's Day soon followed, then *The Worshipbook* in 1970 (containing the rubric "It is fitting . . ." from the *Directory*), a new *Directory for Worship* in 1989 following reunion of the Presbyterian Church in the United States (PCUS) and the United Presbyterian Church in the United States of America (UPCUSA) with a similar exhortation ("It is appropriate . . ."), and, after a series of Supplemental Liturgical Resources, the most recent version of the *Book of Common Worship* (1993), all presuming a weekly service of Word and Sacrament as best practice. The same sorts of critique of practice that are displayed in the changes of Vatican Council II and in the revisions of the *Directory* are equally evident not only in the *Book of Common Worship* but also in the service books of other denominations, including the United Church of Christ, the United Methodist Church, the Evangelical Lutheran Church in America, and the Episcopal Church.

Although weekly Communion is still the exception in the PCUSA, the percentage of congregations that celebrates the Sacrament only quarterly has declined to a small minority (14.9 percent), while 69.3 percent celebrate it monthly, and 71.1 percent report that they also add to their scheduled Communion Sundays the celebrations of the big days on the calendar of the Christian year. Communion may also be celebrated weekly during certain liturgical seasons. The critique of what had become traditional Presbyterian

---

10. *DW* 1961, 211.2

practice, if we mark as the takeoff point the General Assembly's approval of the 1961 *Directory*, has had an escalating effect ever since, measured by a gradual increase in the frequency of celebrating the meal alongside the Word.[11]

Is it time, then, for those who have been laboring to restore the unity of Word and Sacrament every Lord's Day to take a bow, to receive applause for what has been, in retrospect, a remarkable achievement over the last fifty years? Are we done now? Are we now sufficiently reformed? Or, is it possible that there exists no cutoff date for any reforming critique in and for the church, but that reform is a glorious work that is never done?

Something New Is Happening

Ecclesia reformata is never going to be finished with *semper reformanda* (i.e., "always being reformed") as long as history lasts. We stand, as has been noted, in the early years of a new, post-Enlightenment historical era, frequently denominated as postmodern; and whether we have personally felt the effects of crossing that imprecisely drawn frontier or not, the signals have changed. While we must not reject the Enlightenment and that era's many gifts to the human race, it has played itself out, and something new is in formation, and those born since roughly the mid-twentieth century do not have to learn about it in a book or even know about it, since it is for them the air they breathe and the sea in which they swim.

The PCUSA and its predecessors adapted very well to earlier eras, including the so-called Age of Reason (the Enlightenment), and we can adapt again now that the landmarks have been changed. It is not a matter of rejecting the past four hundred years but of taking the good they have brought while moving on. In short, the new era reveals that the church is utterly dependent on the incarnate Word, Jesus Christ, but not on words alone. It is time to rediscover that we are embodied beings, just as the holy God became embodied in Christ.

There is no such thing as a church without ritual. Presbyterians, who may imagine that a 1940s-style, words-based service of song, Scripture, offering, prayer, and sermon involves no ritual, is, in fact, a ritual, a pattern of doing things that is repeated. Even a Quaker meeting has a ritual. An academic discipline called ritual studies has developed in recent times,

---

11. Presbyterian Church (USA), *Clerk's Annual Questionnaire*.

and offers a better understanding of how what we do in worship matters as much or more than what we say.

The modern (Enlightenment) era accented the use of rational discourse, framed in human language, but had less respect for rite and, in fact, was often suspicious of rite. Ritual is also a form of language—body language executed by posture, gesture, movement, and action, accompanied by words. The Presbyterian traditions most familiar to us often exhibit a culturally conventional suspicion of rite—a suspicion that has been nurtured in the now centuries-old "modern" era from which the whole culture is now recovering. Ritual is popularly derided as simply rote repetition that bypasses the heart and the mind. It can be that, of course, just as a sermon can be a form of words that says little, or says much while little is heard or embraced; but neither rite nor preaching can be dismissed so easily.

What is ritual? Ritual may be any pattern of behavior that involves repetition, including brushing one's teeth or loading the dishwasher. Ritual is the menu at Thanksgiving or decorating the tree at Christmas. The virtue of a repeated pattern is that after the first or first few times we become free of the need to think about the details required in executing it. Someone has said that we're not dancing until we don't need to count the steps. Once the dance is internalized, we lose ourselves (or find ourselves) in the dance itself, freed from having to think through every move. Ritual is like the dance. It is something to be realized in the doing, not in thinking about it. We think about it afterwards, or beforehand, or both. But in the midst of the rite, it is counterproductive to think oneself through it, straining to remember and sort out in our conscious minds what every movement, every action, every element might symbolize or represent.

Worship as Theological Formation

The PCUSA is theologically serious but inconsistently so. Inconsistently because, while we value theology, and even have denominational standards that draw a direct line that leads from doctrine to liturgical form, it is nevertheless the case that in practice our church is liturgically laissez-faire. Local congregations are much freer to ignore liturgical guidelines than polity guidelines. The presbytery will require that Session minutes follow a certain form, be examined regularly and approved; but it is difficult to imagine that a presbytery will ever critique a congregation's liturgical practice. And yet, over time, what is said and done in worship is more than just an expression of a theology. It also shapes and forms congregations theologically, thus playing a crucial role in mentoring the faithful either in the church's theology or in some other.

Sacramental acts combine words and body language. They are theology embodied in a unity of speech and action, whether it be the theology we officially profess or another theology altogether, even one that it has not been our intention to espouse or represent. When we make use of liturgical texts such as those found in the *Book of Common Worship*, we discover that rites for both Baptism and Eucharist embody texts and actions that are rooted in Scripture and in the authoritative teaching of our church. The presiding minister may use the texts and follow the rubrics exactly as printed, or create her own extempore language based on the shape and contents of the Thanksgiving over the Water and the Great Thanksgiving as detailed both in the *Directory for Worship* and in the *Book of Common Worship*. Either way, these rites lead the congregation into an encounter with scriptural texts and images that is intended to serve as a means by which the faithful meet and are nourished by the one who is Lord of both Scripture and church. They are a form of resistance to "dumbing down," to borrow a phrase from Marva Dawn.[12] While not requiring worshipers to become academic theologians, the Sacraments embodied in word and action do make it clear that the gospel invites us into a rich complexity that is also utterly simple: "Jesus loves me; this I know, for the Bible tells me so" about sums it up, as Karl Barth said. But there is even in these simple words an invitation to explore, to go deeper, to taste, and enjoy.

Brant Copeland, pastor of First Presbyterian Church in Tallahassee, believes that eucharistic prayers such as the Great Thanksgivings in the *Book of Common Worship* serve to clarify to congregations where the church stands. "Especially as the culture becomes more diverse and we become more sensitive to other faith traditions, there is a kind of tendency on the part of liberal-thinking Protestants to become syncretistic, and I think that is a huge danger—to lose this sort of christocentric, Trinitarian identity—and then we don't have anything to contribute to the conversation. We are just in a sort of spiritual miasma with everybody else, and that's not just a failure of conversation, but of pastoral care as well."

Particularly when classical forms are followed, whether precisely or freely, the Sacraments counter the pressure to reduce the gospel to an oversimplified argument or a sentimental appeal. The Sacraments have to do

---

12. Dawn, *Reaching Out*.

with death and resurrection; with creation and new creation; with Christ in past, present, and future tenses. The Sacraments are both profound and at the same time entirely accessible to adults, children, the mentally challenged, and those for whom dementia has clouded the mind. They are always as utterly simple and as richly complex as life and history inevitably are both. Experienced over time, they shape and reshape us and our communal life in the church, embedding in our conscious and unconscious selves the affirmations otherwise spelled out in our carefully reasoned theology. Will celebrating the Sacrament of the Table more frequently bring the numbers up, restore the heady years when a few mainline churches dominated the religious landscape? Not likely. But they can lead us toward spiritual health and wholeness. The Lord's Supper as a meeting with and union with the risen Christ is itself a standing critique of traditional Presbyterian practice.

In the medieval church, preaching did not disappear, and strong and effective preachers existed, but it declined in frequency. One could easily attend Mass regularly on Sunday without hearing much preaching, and the quality of it was likely to be low since many priests were scarcely literate. Parallel to the decline of preaching was the decline of eucharistic practice. Yes, the Mass was celebrated every Sunday, but often without communicants, and superstitious ideas about the Sacrament flourished. It comes as no surprise that the Reformers believed strongly that the Sacraments needed to be accompanied by the Word. The Word combated superstition so that Baptism and Eucharist might be rightly understood as gifts from God, by whose Spirit the crucified and risen Christ becomes present to the church as its ark, its exodus, its Jordan, and its true spiritual nourishment.

A Church that Loses the Word . . .

The late Howard Hageman, a minister of the Reformed Church in America and one of the writers for the former Southern Church's remarkably successful Covenant Life Curriculum, has brought a critique to our practice that is still relevant. He writes, "A church that loses the Word must finally lose the Sacrament. But is it not equally true that a church which loses the Sacrament must finally lose the Word?"[13] His argument is that when the norm is for the Eucharist to be absent from worship, the result will be a distortion of the Word (i.e., preaching). When the Lord's Day service almost

---

13. Hageman, *Pulpit and Table*, 115.

always centers exclusively around the Word understood literally as words, something happens to preaching, and it is not good.

Although preaching is a unique form of verbal presentation, in the absence of the Sacrament it can easily morph into one of many other kinds of verbal presentation. It can become a lecture on religious topics, therapy for the congregation, therapy for the preacher, Bible study, editorializing, fanciful oratory with no particular point, problem solving, fundraising, or generic motivational speaking, among other things. Although lectionary preaching has become much more common since Presbyterians pioneered in the adoption of the Common Lectionary (now the Revised Common Lectionary), it is unfortunately the case that it is still quite possible to get a sermon idea from a text without actually engaging the text, or even to engage a text while apparently missing the Lord of the text.

Miroslav Volf, a professor at Yale Divinity School who grew up the son of a Pentecostal preacher in Croatia, has lamented the way the absence of the Eucharist affects the service of the Word. It was not that the preaching in the mainline American churches he attended was necessarily unskilled or even unbiblical, but rather that he was "disturbed by the failure of many preachers to make the center of the Christian faith the center of their proclamation." Of course, it is unfortunately the fact, as Volf notes, that some ministers "feel as entitled to redesign the Sacraments as they feel inclined to avoid the cross of Christ. But where the Sacraments are left intact, they point straight back to Christ's self-giving on the cross." Volf found himself, for his own spiritual nourishment, compelled to seek out weekly Eucharist, testifying that "through the celebration of the Eucharist we are made into the body of Christ—for our own salvation and for the salvation of the world . . . By drawing the church back to the cross of Christ, the Eucharist furnishes the church with resources to resist the injustice, deceitfulness and violence that mark the world for which Christ died."[14]

When the Word is not accompanied by the Sacrament, we run the risk of failing to understand that preaching is, in the Reformed tradition, meant to be "sacramental." In other words, it is meant to become a vessel of the Holy Spirit by which ordinary human words become a means by which the living Christ becomes present to his people. Preaching, in effect, has the same object as the Sacraments. Preaching works when the Spirit manifests the crucified and risen Christ through a human being in human speech that is linked to Scripture and prayer, while the Sacraments work when the

---

14. Volf, "Proclaiming the Lord's Death."

Spirit manifests the crucified and risen Christ by means of water, bread, and wine joined to prayer, words, and actions. Is not one or the other sufficient, then? Apparently not, judging by the experience of the medieval church and the experience of a broad swath of Protestants for whom the meal is only occasional.

Hageman believes that the absence of the Lord's Supper in Reformed services most of the time has helped to make Reformed churches "fertile soil for the growth of sectarianism, producing one schism after another in their history."[15] His argument is that by normally isolating Word from Sacrament, Reformed churches have tended to intellectualize the gospel, which can easily lead to the belief that it is both possible and desirable to base our unity on a rather too closely defined agreement of minds. Of course, under the stress of contemporary polarization around political and social issues, we have seen Episcopalians splintering too even though they typically practice weekly Eucharist. Nevertheless, in the longer stretches of history Anglicans come nowhere near the Reformed as champion splitters. Elizabeth Deibert of Peace Presbyterian Church, describing her pastoral experience, says, "I firmly believe that weekly Sacrament with the Word keeps the congregation grounded in the mystery of 'Immanuel,' and preserves the peace, unity, and purity of the congregation."

But What about the Sermon?

The expectation, every Sunday, that we are being led toward the meal has an effect on preaching, whether from the point of view of the preacher or the point of view of those listening to the sermon. Vice Moderator Tom Trinidad of Faith Church in Colorado Springs testifies that weekly Communion has helped to make his preaching more focused. Both he and the congregation know and expect that the sermon is preaching "toward the Table" every week.

Like the Luke 24 Emmaus Road passage, "I'm taking the congregation on an evangelical journey, interpreting the scriptures around Christ and then breaking bread with them." Trinidad has been experimenting with splitting the sermon into four pieces: teaching, preaching, sealing, and serving.

> The way it connects with the way evangelicals outside the Reformed tradition do is that I start before the reading with some

---

15. Hageman, *Pulpit and Table*, 115.

teaching—a brief, one- to two-minute introduction to the context and background of the text—then go to what we in the Reformed tradition would call a proclamation of the Word; and then I wait until after the prayers and offertory, and offer from the Table the last part of the sermon as it relates to the Sacrament, and that is the "sealing" part of it; and then hold off the last part—what the evangelicals would call the "application"—until a kind of extended Charge and Benediction, the "serving" part.

Fred Anderson, pastor of Madison Avenue Presbyterian Church, believes that preaching every Sunday in a eucharistic context has affected his preaching dramatically. Anderson observes that "if I'm preaching from an Old Testament text, I don't suddenly have to find Christ under every rock." He can let the Old Testament text speak on its own, "with the kind of integrity it needs," because he knows that "before the service is over, the Christian gospel will be authentically proclaimed in the eucharistic prayer."

In Austin, the pastor at the New Covenant Fellowship, James Lee, senses that there is a kind of reciprocal relationship between sermon and meal. "At some point," he suggests, "there has to be a place in the sermon that leads to Communion, and in the Communion a place that speaks to the sermon." At times, Lee reflects, the responsibility of preaching, of handling holy things, seems so large that he feels unworthy, and then the gift of the Supper reminds him that none of it is about him or what he is able to give, but "it's about who God is and who I am in the Lord."

Chuck Mendenhall of the Lake Travis Church has become much more intentional in linking the sermon and the Sacrament. "There is a sense," he says, "in which the Word impacts people on a metalevel" in a way he had not discovered in years of worshiping without weekly Eucharist. He believes that the presence of the meal every week "really does enhance people's experience of the Word."

The pastor at Pine Street Presbyterian Church in Harrisburg, Russell Sullivan, wants it understood that in that congregation neither he nor whoever is preaching shortens the sermon, as though it were necessary to do that with Communion to follow. In weekly-Eucharist churches, there is, indeed, a full sermon, and not that abbreviated version that has so often been titled a meditation in congregations that celebrate the meal occasionally but not every Sunday.

"Instead of coming to our church and listening to a sermon, you can be part of the sermon," says Jim Walker of the Hot Metal Bridge community in Pittsburgh. In HMB's mission statement, one objective is, "'proclamation of the Word of God.' We wanted people to participate in the Word of God, so we put together a creative-arts team, to help young adults not just listen to a sermon but become the proclaimers of the sermon."

The co-pastors, Walker and Jeff Eddings, met as theater majors in college more than twenty years ago, and started a theater company while they served as youth ministers in different churches. At HMB, they use drama to proclaim the Word. Most of the dramas, according to an article in the *Wall Street Journal*, "explore Bible themes flavored with pop culture and modern-day skepticism. 'Sticking With Fishing' ponders what would have happened had Peter not dropped his net to follow Jesus. Elijah joins a man on the ledge thinking about a last leap. The archangel Gabriel kills time as he awaits news of Christ's birth."[16] Jason Sluka, a twenty-eight-year-old alcoholic and cocaine addict, was present at worship to see a drama in which Eddings played a man in jail grappling with demons. "He made me bawl my eyes out," says Sluka, who became part of a treatment program at the Salvation Army.[17] Being part of the sermon leads directly to the Table.

When Word and Eucharist are held together, the Word interprets the Sacrament, and the Sacrament interprets the Word, sometimes explicitly, more often subtly. Will such a practice draw a crowd? Bring the numbers up? It would be risky to make such an optimistic prediction. But it does bring together what belongs together, keeping both preaching and the meal anchored in the gospel so that both may nourish the faithful with spiritual food desperately needed so that we may keep the faith in a world that is frequently indifferent to it.

A Learned Thanks-Giving

Restoring the broken unity of Word and Sacrament matters because an honest, biblically based critique of our worship would remind us that thanksgiving must be at the heart of our worshiping assemblies, and not left either to chance or to once a month or even less frequently. The Greek word *eucharistein* means to thank, or give thanks. From it comes the ancient word *Eucharist* to describe the Lord's Supper, and it is an appropriate name for our sacred meal. In the New Testament, the sequence of four verbs that signal a eucharistic link is *taking, blessing, breaking,* and *giving*; but *blessing* is sometimes *giving thanks*, and the two seem to be interchangeable.

16. Sataline, "Church Uses Drama to Draw New Crowd."
17. Ibid.

As I noted earlier, when Justin Martyr describes early Christian worship in the second century, he describes the presentation of bread and wine, and describes the presiding officer offering up "prayers and thanksgivings." Christian worship might be described, in part at least, as a weekly exercise in being thankful.

Thankfulness comes naturally when something good happens: we fall in love, get a promotion, receive recognition for some accomplishment, get a good report from the doctor, are given great, hard-to-get tickets to the concert or game. We feel gratitude, even if it is not always immediately clear to whom we owe our thanks. But feelings of thankfulness last only for a little while, and then we revert to a more typical, everyday mode of wishing that we had more of something or other, or that a break might come our way. To learn to live a eucharistic life does not mean seeing the world through rose-colored glasses, pasting a smile on our faces and pretending to be cheerful no matter what. The eucharistic life has nothing to do with positive thinking, or suppressing perfectly normal feelings that are part of life, such as lament, regret, anger, and indignation—healthy examples of which can be found in Scripture. Rather, it is a matter of learning how to lay a foundation of gratitude that undergirds all the shifting emotional states common to human experience.

Brian Gerrish writes that "what becomes clearer in the final edition of Calvin's *Institutes* is that the father's liberality and his children's answering gratitude, or lack of it, is not only the theme of the Lord's Supper but a fundamental theme, perhaps the most fundamental theme, of an entire system of theology."[18] It is possible, and even sometimes happens, that prayers of thanksgiving are offered in services of the Word, and the *Book of Common Worship* provides for one even in the absence of the Lord's Supper. However, thanksgiving is easily forgotten or hurried over, whereas the Eucharist is itself an act of thanksgiving, not only registered with the ears, but enacted bodily. Over time, it can form a community into a eucharistic shape. Thanksgiving is so important and so essential for spiritual formation in a Christian sense that it deserves a place alongside the Word in every Lord's Day service, and in the Eucharist it is inescapable.

But will it increase the number of new members? Will it bring back those halcyon days when a portrait of the Moderator of our General Assembly might actually appear on the cover of a national magazine? Not necessarily. But what it is likely to do is to strengthen the foundations,

---

18. Gerrish, *Grace and Gratitude*, 20

clarify who we are and whose we are in a time when Presbyterians, other Protestants, and Christians generally have to learn how to understand ourselves to be a minority, if not yet numerically, then certainly culturally. What has providentially been given to the church is a gift to be received and welcomed gratefully in a time of rapid cultural change, in which Presbyterians and other Christian sisters and brothers have to learn more carefully and more intentionally what it means to be a people gathered around Jesus Christ in a society that, for the most part, does not identify itself in relation either to Christ or his church.

Iona's Gift

George MacLeod, a minister of the Church of Scotland, initiated the founding of the Iona Community in Scotland in 1938. Most American Presbyterians know it as a community housed in the restored buildings of an ancient monastic community located on the island of Iona, off the west coast of Scotland, but it is more than that. MacLeod, who was serving as a pastor in Glasgow, became concerned because the Church of Scotland was no longer reaching working-class people, of whom there were many in Glasgow and in other Scottish factory or shipbuilding-towns. He gathered others to work with him in a project that involved both the restoration of the Iona buildings and also inner-city ministry, while rethinking the worship practices of the established church so as to make it more accessible to people accustomed to working with their hands and backs.

The worship of the Scottish Kirk was simple and austere, and for those assembled, mostly involved listening to the minister pray and preach. MacLeod felt led to restore the Sacrament to its rightful place alongside the sermon every Lord's Day, believing that it offered another way for people to meet, receive, and welcome Jesus Christ—one not so heavily dependent on skill at decoding language. The result was the formation of a Christian community based both on Iona and in the inner city of Glasgow, and those who come to Iona on the Lord's Day will find that weekly Communion, as well as preaching, is their practice.

It is sometimes noted that Presbyterians are the Jesuits of Protestantism. The comparison is meant to be a compliment in that Jesuits are noted for their intellectual life. The Presbyterian/Reformed tradition is indeed one that has nourished an enormous amount of scholarship, including serious biblical and theological scholarship, over the centuries since the

Reformation, and Presbyterians set high standards for the intellectual preparation of our ministers, so perhaps the comparison with the Jesuits is apt. And yet, truth be told, it probably overstates the case. Of course, sometimes at worship it becomes apparent that we are sitting in a thoughtful community in which the gospel is presented in a way that takes seriously the learning of the world as well as the learning of the church, and many of us are grateful to find a place in which the life of the mind is respected. As glorious as that is for some, at least, such worship may seem to exclude those for whom deep thought about the faith does not come as easily, or to bypass equally earnest folk for whom encountering Christ and celebrating his gospel requires respect for other senses than the sense of hearing only, as well as to marginalize children.

The most common remedies seem to be either to pare down the sermon to the point of oversimplification, or to turn it into some sort of Hallmark moment. Another way might be to follow where Lord MacLeod and the Iona community set out to lead us: in addition to thoughtful preaching, to restore the missing Sacrament, honoring the body, respecting the other senses and helping us find their rightful place alongside the sense of hearing. Calvin comments that it is no accident that Jesus commanded, in John 6, that we eat his flesh and drink his blood, but that it is by choosing these words that he shows "that no one should think that the life that we receive from him is received by mere knowledge."[19]

James Lee, of Austin's New Covenant Fellowship, observes that "the question was how we could, theologically, move from once a month to weekly. The answer seemed to come from Jesus: 'As often as you do this, you do it in remembrance of me.' It became a way for people to hang their hats on that. It was a way of remembering, celebrating, and reflecting on the risen Savior."

---

19. *Institutes* 4.17.5, 1365.

Three

Problems, Obstacles, and Opportunities

If one were to take a survey of a few knowledgeable Presbyterians, asking each what they believe most faithfully describes the greatest strength of Presbyterianism, it is likely that the questioner would get as many different responses as there are responders. Each would see as characteristic of our tradition that which she or he most values in it. And, it is also probable that each would be in a position to make a strong case in support of their opinions. This is true, not because we are particularly confused, but because the Presbyterian and Reformed traditions are richly layered.

When Stated Clerk Eugene Carson Blake helped to initiate the Consultation on Church Union in 1960, the stated goal was to bring together several churches to form a new one that would be "catholic, evangelical, and reformed." It is possible, in my view, to see our own PCUSA and the larger Reformed tradition as containing within itself all three of these characteristics. We are catholic, we are evangelical, and we are reformed (and "being reformed")—each characteristic rooted in the Reformation itself. At different times and places some of these descriptions are more evident and more vivid than in others, but they are all present in the larger tradition. Of course, each of these descriptors—catholic, evangelical, and reformed—is, in itself, rich, nuanced, and complex.

Another way to understand Presbyterianism, in all of these versions, is as a tradition that places a high value on thinking things through with as much care and precision as possible. Our church's contemporary position has been described by some as a generous orthodoxy. Generous in the sense that we make room for diversity and do not value the use of coercion to force everybody to think exactly alike, or at least to pretend that they do. More often than not, we welcome questions, we understand that people are at different stages of growth in the Christian life and in their understanding of it, and our requirements for membership are grounded in a simple confession of faith in Christ as Lord (which is no small thing) rather than in a blanket endorsement of a whole theological corpus. Alongside the word *generous* is the word *orthodoxy*, referring not to twentieth-century quarrels over the nature of biblical authority but rather to the core affirmations of the classical tradition of the church in its ecumenical and Reformed incarnations.

Our church is one that takes seriously its responsibility to serve as a mentor to its members. Calvin, following Augustine, referred to the church as a kind of "mother," no doubt having in mind its obligation to nurture and guide. We have a polity—a way of governing and of dealing with inevitable conflict—and we have a *Book of Confessions* that is a collection of creeds, confessions, and catechisms originating in different times and places that is meant to serve as a guide to thought and reflection rather than a straitjacket. In confessions from different generations and countries there is both discontinuity—they do not all agree in every detail—and a general, and larger continuity. In other words, they all seem to be somewhat different dialects of a common mother tongue. We do not say to each individual Christian, or even to each separate congregation: figure it out for yourself. Rather, as a teaching church, we have a tradition to set before ourselves, our officers, our new members, and seekers. That tradition is one of a high theology, a high Christology, a high doctrine of the Holy Trinity, and also a high doctrine of the church and the Sacraments.

Tradition?

Reformed people, as well as Protestants generally, have sometimes disparaged tradition, as though tradition and the Bible were two entirely distinct sources competing for an authoritative position in the church. If that were true, it would seem to be transparently the case that it would be imperative to choose the Bible over tradition. However, it is not the case that Protestants grant no authority to tradition. First of all, the Bible itself is a distillation of the tradition that was first passed down in oral forms, whether as remembered narratives, prophetic utterances, testimony, preaching, or catechesis. Second, Christians of every generation are heirs of all the preceding generations, who have preserved and handed on not only doctrine and practices, but also the Bible itself, including memories of how Scripture has been read and understood in different times and places. Every time the preacher or church-school teacher consults a Bible commentary, they are encountering a long tradition of thoughtful reading and interpretation.

Further, Reformed Christians of the early twenty-first century are heirs of all our Christian forebears and of the historic decisions they have felt led to make as they have encountered new occasions, questions, and circumstances, from Nicaea and Chalcedon to the various Reformation confessions to the Westminster Confession or the Theological Declaration of Barmen or the Confession of 1967. In short, Presbyterians not only have a tradition, but they honor it and understand it to be authoritative, although not infallible, and meant always to be understood as subordinate to Scripture and subject to possible reform.

For this rich tradition we must be thankful, for without such an anchor it is very easy for a church to surrender entirely to whatever is in fashion, whether a fashion of the moment or one that has dominated a whole culture for a long period of time, such as the "modern" (post-Enlightenment) era now ending. The church always adapts to current circumstances, as well it must, but it is well at the same time to take a long view, which includes learning from its own past. No heresy ever goes away entirely. It just resurfaces under other names, to be marketed as though it were a new insight—the next, coming thing.

Presbyterians run into at least two problems when it comes to dealing with tradition: 1) it is tempting to imagine that nothing that happened in the church between the closing of the New Testament canon and the sixteenth century Reformation needs to be consulted or taken too seriously; and 2) it is easy to grant the greatest authority to the most recent and most familiar tradition.

With respect to problem number one: the Reformers did not imagine themselves to be starting a new church, or restarting a church that had not existed since New Testament times. They understood their work to be a reform movement within the one universal church, committed to scrutinizing and critiquing contemporary practice (and the theology that supported that practice) in a particular context, in the light of Scripture. In other words, they might have disagreed with decisions made in and by the church in the past, or with practices instituted, but they did not imagine that the church had ceased to exist whenever it had made an unfortunate turn. Nor did they imagine that the medieval church as they knew it was the only form of church that existed between New Testament times and their own. Calvin, for example, was a student of the early church fathers, many of whom were major figures for the Orthodox churches of the East and often for the church in the West as well, and he cited them as authorities in support of his reforms. Like Calvin, we can and must consider ourselves part of the broader church, the ecumenical church.

With respect to the second problem, if it was possible for the church to make mistakes before the Reformation, it was also possible to make mistakes during and after the Reformation, right up to this moment. And, if the most recent tradition is simply "the way we have always done it," then we risk enshrining practice that will not easily withstand scrutiny historically, theologically, pastorally, or even practically. In other words, what is called for in a church that is willing to be reformed, when necessary, according to the word of God, is a view that is both broad and long. Such a church understands itself to be a part of the whole church, heirs of both the good and the bad, all that preceded the Reformation as well as what followed, and to be willing to learn from sisters and brothers in the past as well as the present, and from the ecumenical church as well as our own particular ecclesiastical tradition. Though far too often Presbyterians have been in practice both schismatic and sectarian, as part of the Reformed tradition we are nevertheless in the fortunate position of being genetically ecumenical, following the lead of our Reformers.

Is it the duty of contemporary Presbyterians, Lutherans, and Methodists to discover exactly what Calvin, Luther, or Wesley did and re-create their churches today? Although a few might advocate for that, they are not many. Contemporary Christians, whatever their confession, cannot re-create a version of themselves that was frozen in time at the moment of their origin, as though the critiques and proposed solutions that met the needs of an earlier reforming era should be relevant to every other circumstance and context until the end of time. Nor should any of the churches imagine that their basic integrity rises or falls with the ability to justify whatever their current practice might have come to be.

Which Tradition?

When it comes to actual eucharistic practice, our Presbyterian predicament is that we are often in the position of defending only the narrowest slice of our tradition, which is most likely to be whatever we have been repeatedly exposed to in our lifetimes. The sixteenth-century Reformers made enormous strides under difficult conditions, but the heritage they left for us is not always the heritage they intended to leave. So it is that the twenty-first-century church has inherited the practice of infrequent Communion (infrequent even when it is monthly), a practice that originated by happenstance rather than principle. Decisions made in response to a cultural/historical moment in sixteenth-century Geneva, or practices developed in post-Reformation Scotland under the conditions of a severe shortage of ministers have become institutionalized and unquestioned rather than understood as temporary and expedient adjustments.

In other cases, our Reformers left us their best insights, but the task was so overwhelming that they could not successfully identify every point at which medieval practice needed to be challenged. Pre-Reformation practice was to present the Eucharist as though it were a reward for those pious few who had already cleansed their consciences and their souls by a process of self-examination and repentance beforehand. In altered form, this conception of the meal persisted in the churches of the Reformation. The resulting perception that it was necessary to guard the Table from the unworthy led to practices of preparation that eventually became perceived as arbitrary and judgmental, and also, because they are time-consuming, tedious and difficult to sustain.

American Presbyterians no longer expect the elders of the church to visit in homes to examine the worthiness of potential communicants, distributing tokens to those who pass the test; nor do we provide preparatory services communicants are required to attend before a Communion service. Nevertheless, these practices, though mostly long forgotten, have left in their wake the sense that the Lord's Supper is a somber affair, far from a "joyful feast." This legacy of the medieval Mass, a legacy radically reconsidered by the Roman Church following the Second Vatican Council, nevertheless continues to influence Presbyterian practice by the way it has persisted in shaping the tone of the Communion service, a tone reinforced and perpetuated by everything from the accompanying music to the expectation that one must sit still in quiet, personal reflection, not meeting the eyes of others—a communal event that is, nevertheless, somehow private. It is about something that happened a long time ago more than about something that is happening now or something anticipated to happen in the future. It more nearly resembles a replay of the *Last* Supper than it resembles the first *Lord's* Supper on the road to Emmaus on Easter evening or the promised Messianic banquet. We are more likely to find ourselves on the way to Gethsemane, as though since the *Last* Supper preceded the resurrection, we are not yet permitted to turn our eyes toward the empty tomb and the risen Lord or to the promise of Christ's coming kingdom for which the resurrection serves as both promise and downpayment.

A Pennsylvania pastor tells the story of a retired Presbyterian minister he encountered at the door after a Christmas Eve service at which the congregation had celebrated the Lord's Supper. The retired minister was scandalized, deeply offended that the church would have Communion on what was supposed to be a joyful occasion! One need not look too far to find among us this deeply rooted sense that the holy meal and a joyful occasion are two separate, distinct, and incompatible things. Surely this way of looking at the meal is dying out, isn't it? And yet, even with a *Directory for Worship* that reflects a deeper and more biblical scholarship, and a *Book of Common Worship* that embodies it in texts and rubrics, the actual experience of the Lord's Supper in many Presbyterian congregations still resembles something more like a memorial service than a meeting with the crucified and risen Christ.[1]

When Steve Montgomery became pastor of Idlewild Church in Memphis, he found that the practice there was quarterly Communion on Sundays plus Maundy Thursday and Christmas Eve. In the first year of his pastorate, he asked the Worship and Music Committee if they would be willing to study the Lord's Supper with him. He led them in a discussion that included a close look at the meaning of the Lord's Supper, an overview of Reformed Sacramental theology, and Calvin's thought. What he discovered was that most of the congregation had learned to think of the Lord's Supper as basically "a funeral, with no idea of it being any kind of eucharistic feast."

What Presbyterians take to be normative is an inherited set of practices in search of a theology, or at least in search of a principled reason that underlies and supports what is familiar. Perhaps the reasoning might be that since these are the practices we have, they must be the practices we

---

1. Moore-Keish, *Do This*.

are meant to have, and so surely there must be, somewhere, a principle to justify them. As one pastor has put it, "in the absence of a positive affirmation of the Eucharist in communicating the risen Christ to his disciples, people in the pews have attached positive meaning to the *absence* of the Eucharist."[2]

Obstacles to Reform: No Longer "Special"

And what might that positive meaning be? Pressed to discover a positive meaning, the most typical Presbyterian response is likely to be, "Well, Pastor, if we have Communion more often, it just won't be 'special.'" Although the protest that weekly (or even monthly) Communion will be simply too frequent to be special is not an argument that can be easily defended on theological grounds, it is nevertheless one that needs to be taken seriously. As Fred Anderson points out, the worship life of the congregation is likely to be a person's "central point of identity with the church." For good or for ill, the piety of many Presbyterians has been formed around occasional Communion practiced in a manner that is basically introspective rather than celebrative, focusing on Christ's sacrificial death on the cross with little or no notice of his resurrection. For those whose Christian life has been shaped by this practice, the point of the rite is not what the Spirit gives in the rite itself, but the rite is a device meant to provoke thinking about its underlying meaning in order to kindle certain emotions.

There are several reasons for this way of perceiving a sacramental action, but one is certainly the accent on remembering. After all, the Lord said, "Do this in remembrance of me," and those words are often inscribed on our Communion Tables or on the cloths that cover them. The act of remembering seems to require an intense effort to direct our thoughts to a past event, the betrayal and death of Jesus Christ, now absent. In other words, the sacramental action is meant to be translated into thought—perhaps thought about Christ's sacrifice, perhaps thought about the need for and promise of forgiveness of sin, but, in any case, an exercise in reflective thinking. The unspoken presumption is that nothing can happen in the Sacrament unless we make it happen by focusing our thought so as to arouse the appropriate feelings. This is actually rather strenuous work, and more easily undertaken at widely separated intervals rather than frequently. But in Scripture, the remembrance is in the *doing*: the taking of bread and wine,

2. Copeland, *Eucharist*, 21.

giving thanks, breaking the bread, distributing it, eating and drinking. Remembering is not a psychological act. Furthermore, the sacramental action is also a prayer that *God* may remember (so to speak) Christ crucified and risen and so keep the divine promise of a new creation made in Christ's resurrection. The Bible includes many instances in which the prayers of the people exhort God to remember: for instance, "Remember your congregation, which you acquired long ago, which you redeemed to be the tribe of your heritage" (Ps 74:2). The experience of the wider church has been that it is not we but the Triune God who is the chief actor in the Sacrament, by means of the Holy Spirit, and that we are the beneficiaries of the gift, which is the presence of Christ himself.

When someone claims to be afraid of losing something "special," they are expressing a fear that frequency will make the meal routine enough that people will stop thinking about what they are doing, and since it is the thinking that makes it meaningful, the emotional responses that we associate with the Sacrament will be lost. In other words, they fear that more frequent Communion will not be a gain, but a loss.

Of course, it is quite possible to explain that the fear of loss rests on a misunderstanding both of the Sacrament itself and of what a rite is supposed to be and do. It is also possible to cite Scripture and quote Calvin and the *Directory for Worship*, but in the face of the fear of loss, neither explanations nor quoting authoritative sources is likely to make much difference. The resistance offered under the fear of losing something "special" is more likely to yield to a pastoral response than one that piles up evidence sufficient to win an argument. Such a response might be something like, "Come and see."

"Come and see" may begin with something as simple as introducing new information followed by a long-term give-and-take without any motion being on the table. People are typically less likely to feel threatened and more open to discussion when there is no vote pending.

There is more than one way for something to be special. Will weekly Communion make it less special? The answer is that it will replace one kind of special with another. What some would call special about the practice of relatively infrequent Communion is that, since it varies from the norm, it introduces a periodic change of tempo and tone. For example, it is not uncommon for people to imagine that worship is most meaningful when it is associated with an emotional high, achievable in moments of high drama. Maundy Thursday, in its own way, is special. Good Friday is special. And yet, as much as we may need and appreciate them, it is too much for us to transport ourselves back to Maundy Thursday and Good Friday every Sunday, or even every month, lest the good news seem to be only bad news. Maundy Thursday and Good Friday become good news only in the context of the whole story, which must include Easter.

Those who actually experience Communion weekly discover a different sort of specialness about it. Describing his experience of Eucharist in the chapel at St. Andrew's University in Scotland, Presbyterian pastor Brant Copeland tells of his discovery. "There, at his Table, I met the risen Christ. Before I had learned the jargon of the academic theologian, I experienced the risen Christ through Eucharistic celebration . . . I experienced this 'Eucharistic lens' as a gift of pure grace. I did not achieve it through any spiritual or intellectual effort. I simply received it as a gift. I was invited to eat and drink with other disciples at the Table of the risen Lord, and 'he was known to [us] in the breaking of the bread.'"[3] Experience trumps arguments. Come and see—something special, every week.

The perception that infrequency heightens the impact of an experience is, interestingly, not carried over into other acts of worship, much less into ordinary daily routines like sitting down with a spouse or friends for a drink before dinner. If infrequency adds meaning, then could it not be proposed that we limit preaching to once a month? Or pray the Lord's Prayer only quarterly? Or perhaps meet for worship only every other week? Worship is a weekly appointment we keep, a discipline we undertake for its own sake and for our own, whatever our emotional temperature at the moment, because it is here, in assembly, that we expect to meet the holy and gracious God.

At Pine Street Church in Harrisburg, an elder who had pressed hardest against weekly Communion on the grounds that it would become too common and too mechanical, its special character lost, changed his mind after twenty years of experience. He reflects that he had never known that "there were so many dimensions to be experienced. Communion is so multidimensional. It is much more than I knew or could imagine. And, each time I come to the table, it is somehow new again."[4] Come and see.

---

3. Copeland, *Eucharist*, 7.
4. Anderson, "Moving toward Every Sunday," part 4, 1–2.

"Too Catholic"

If the most likely objection to weekly Communion is that increasing its frequency will make it less special, then the next is likely to be, "It's too Catholic!" Like the first, this objection is not as likely to be raised by young Presbyterians, but more probably by those who have been Presbyterian for a long time. After all, if we have to discover a rationale for what we are used to, it must be because what we are used to is intended to mark a difference between ourselves and what some other church is used to, and certainly the church from which we have historically most needed to differentiate ourselves is the Roman Catholic Church, isn't it? Again, one could respond facetiously: should we not baptize because the Romans baptize? Not pray the Lord's Prayer, because they do? Not read more than one biblical text at worship, because they do? Not affirm the creed together, since they do?

Current Catholic practice has been in place only since the late 1960s. When our Reformers were forced out of the Roman Church in the sixteenth century, the developing eucharistic practice of the Reformation diverged radically from that of the medieval church, and the differences were hardened by the response of the Council of Trent. The Reformers' intention, though, was not to be different for the sake of being different, but rested on a theologically and biblically based critique of then-current practice. Certainly, wherever we have principled differences with Roman Catholics, we should not be shy about making note of them, presuming that we do it in a charitable and fraternal way and are willing to accept their critiques in turn.

In these days, when Vatican II seems a distant memory, it is not difficult to make a list of issues with which we disagree profoundly with the Roman Catholic Church, beginning with its exclusion of women from ministry and of laypeople from any role in decision making in an all-male hierarchy. However, there are far more similarities between Catholic and Reformed versions of Christianity than differences, and there is no need to accent differences where they are not rooted in principle. For example, getting up and moving at communion was the practice in the churches of both John Calvin and John Knox, neither of whom can be accused of timidity when it came to declaring principled differences with Catholics.

Like the resistance that stems from a fear of losing something special, the fear that weekly Eucharist is too Catholic is not always alleviated by providing information, whether historical, theological, or practical. David Batchelder believes that "it takes leadership that is willing to recognize that it will meet resistance and not be threatened by it and become defensive. The answer, generally, is not better arguments or more historical background, although I think you have to have some of that. You have to explore what lies behind the resistance. To find a way to initiate conversations that will help people to revisit their resistance."

The fear of becoming "too Catholic" is likely to be rooted in some fear or anxiety. Carol Schweitzer, Associate Professor of Pastoral Care at Union Presbyterian Seminary, suggests that a pastoral approach to this objection would be to give the objector an opening to express herself more fully by responding with a question such as, "I'm not sure I understand what you mean when you say 'too Catholic.'" Given a chance to talk it out, one may discover that the objection is rooted in something closer to home, such as the disappointment springing from a child becoming Catholic, or from resentment of an obnoxious neighbor. Or, it may be that the objector was raised in a family that was prejudiced against Catholics, who feels as though she or he owes it to the parental generation to maintain the barriers. Presbyterians who live in a geographic area in which the Roman Church is numerically dominant and forcefully present may be expressing a need for resistance to the larger group by maintaining old distinctions. Sometimes this protest simply means that the person is finding it hard to deal with change in worship.

At First Church in Owensboro, Kentucky, little resistance emerged when worshipers began to experiment with weekly Eucharist, but two women in the church, lifetime friends now in their eighties, raised the objection that the practice was "too Catholic." Both have Catholic sons-in-law, and both have fought attending Baptisms in Catholic churches, and both shared a chronic suspicion of that church. But even old prejudices yield to experience. Now, after five years of weekly Communion at First Presbyterian, the two women are present every Sunday. Both sit in the very back of the sanctuary, one on one side of the center aisle and the other on the opposite side. The congregation comes forward to commune, beginning with the back pews. So, these two women are the first ones to approach the Table, making their way up a long aisle, hand in hand, communing with smiles on their faces.

Of course, to look at this protest from an entirely different angle, the practice of weekly Eucharist will be familiar to Roman Catholics who find themselves, for one reason or another, no longer at home in that church, or for couples in mixed marriages. Several of the churches studied report that lapsed or disaffected Catholics in search of another church home have found themselves attracted to their congregations.

Fred Anderson remembers James White as having said that a good liturgical decision needs to be theologically correct, biblically and liturgically correct, aesthetically correct, and pastorally correct as well. Anderson says, "Always as we have approached liturgical change I have made it clear that we could talk about it. I think often a lot of people's fear is that something is going to be shoved down their throats."

"Won't It Take Too Long?"

Other objections are likely to be entirely practical: "It will make the service too long." This anxiety surfaced in many of the congregations studied. Of course it is true that typical Presbyterian Communion services tend to take a long time. With local variations, it goes like this: After the Great Thanksgiving, the presiding minister gives trays of cut bread to the elders, who then move down the aisles and pass them down the pews. When all have completed the distribution of the bread, the elders gather at the rear and then process to the front of the church where they return the trays to the presiding minister, who places them back on the Communion Table. Then the elders are seated and the minister serves them. Then, the entire process is repeated with the trays holding individual cups. If this process were to become weekly, it would surely lengthen the service, and the service is frequently already lengthened by the addition of things such as the "Moment for Mission," which is rarely as short as a moment (often lasting from seven to ten minutes); a children's sermon or something like time with the children; and sometimes announcements made from the pulpit at the urging of those who are sure that these announcements will be taken more seriously than if read in the printed bulletin; and possibly a period of sharing joys and concerns. Dealing with all these additions is time consuming enough on Sundays when there is no celebration of the Lord's Supper.

Related to the concern with the length of the service is one that sometimes surfaces in relation to preaching. Presbyterians are accustomed, on Communion Sundays, to a much shorter sermon, frequently not even called a sermon but rather a meditation that is likely to be designed specifically for the sacramental occasion. If Communion were to be every Sunday, would that be the end of preaching?

The fact is that it is not. Pastors of churches that celebrate the Eucharist weekly are quite as committed to preaching as any others, and have no wish to sacrifice it, fully persuaded that a vigorous preaching of the Word is not in competition with the Lord's Supper, but actually a part of it and necessary for it. The length of sermons varies in churches with and without weekly Eucharist. At the Church of the Servant, a Christian Reformed Church in Grand Rapids, Michigan, the Lord's Supper is celebrated every week, and the sermon is typically as long as twenty-five to thirty minutes.

Congregational cultures are not all the same, but there are ways to make room for doing what most needs to be done. Fred Anderson quotes an elder from Pine Street Church who had voted against weekly Communion for fear that it would have a negative impact on the sermon. Twenty years later the elder said, "I was wrong. I was dead wrong, and I am happy to acknowledge that . . . Now we are fed both from the pulpit and the table."[5] Come and see. Another elder in the same church had, in the beginning, been concerned about the effect that weekly Communion would have on preaching. Two decades later, after considerable experience with the practice, he was happy to say that a Word and Sacrament service every week had taught him to hear the texts and sermons differently. He said, "Calvin really had it right. It's too bad the city fathers in Geneva never let him do there what we've done here."[6]

A Presbyterian minister who spent more than three decades in pastoral ministry found himself sitting in a pew for ten years after taking an academic position. During all the years of pastoral ministry, he reports that it was rare for people to complain about the length of a service, and on the occasions when it happened, the complaint was usually filed gently. Nevertheless, he presumed that if one or two bothered to register discomfort with the length of the service, there must be dozens more, hundreds more, who felt the same way but failed to speak up. However, when he joined the ranks of people in the pews, he noticed no one checking their watches and heard no complaints from people around him even when the service ran ten, fifteen, twenty minutes longer than expected. In retrospect, the few complaints he had heard over the years seem to have been, in fact, representative of only a few people rather than many.

The larger churches consulted for this study report that with Communion every Sunday their services run about an hour and fifteen minutes. Smaller congregations find that their services may take less time than that.

5. Anderson, "Moving Toward Every Sunday," part 4, 2.
6. Ibid., part 2, 12.

The Mendenhalls at Lake Travis Church in Austin follow the Service for the Lord's Day in the *Book of Common Worship* very closely, and the service can be completed in an hour. The service at Peace Church in Lakewood Ranch, Florida, takes about and hour and five minutes. At First Church in Owensboro, Kentucky, they use a full-blown eucharistic liturgy but have learned how to tighten up the service without giving up substance, and their service is also a few minutes more than an hour. Russell Sullivan of Pine Street Church reports that he had to learn to stop worrying about everything happening within an hour. Quoting the church's minister of music, he said, "I have since learned what Thomas Clark-Jones says, 'Worship is over when it's over.'"[7]

Variations in Practice

Most churches with weekly Communion invite those who are able to leave their seats to go to one or more stations where they will receive the bread and cup. If viewed solely from the standpoint of efficiency, it is certainly less time-consuming for the people to go to the bread and cup rather than taking the elements to them, and it requires fewer people to serve. Some weekly-Eucharist churches use this method almost all the time but occasionally serve the people in their pews. When Faith Presbyterian Church in Colorado Springs first began communing weekly, they continued the practice that was familiar and expected, passing the bread and cup in the pews. After a time, it became obvious that serving was simply taking too much time, so they doubled the number of servers. Now, after a period of experimentation, they provide four stations in a wide center aisle, and the people go to the nearest station, then circle around to return to their seats.

Upper Room Fellowship in Pittsburgh communes with the people seated. The configuration of the worship space is of four sections of chairs, all facing toward the center of the room. They first pass the bread, with two cups following closely behind, one cup with grape juice and one with wine, and people either drink directly from a cup or commune by intinction.

When Second Presbyterian Church in Lexington, Kentucky added an 8:30 a.m. service with weekly Eucharist, they chose to commune by coming forward and gathering in a large circle around the Communion Table, passing the bread followed immediately by the trays of individual cups. As the service grew larger, concentric circles were added. Other churches follow

7. Ibid., part 4, 2.

the same practice as Church of the Servant in Grand Rapids, much like the practice of St. Giles Cathedral in Edinburgh, in which people are directed to come forward to form a circle, then return to their places as succeeding circles are formed until all have been served.

The most common method of communing is by intinction. However, at the 8:30 service at Pine Street in Harrisburg, the bread is broken from a common loaf and placed in the hands of the communicants, who then either dip it into a common cup of grape juice, or consume the bread prior to approaching a server who holds a tray of individual cups with grape juice. In some churches, a broken loaf is offered and the communicant breaks off a piece of bread, while in others, the server breaks the bread and places it in the palm of an open hand. Having the server place the bread in the hand represents that communicants are receiving rather than taking something, and it has the practical advantage that the loaf is touched by only one person. Servers can quietly wash their hands with a sanitizing lotion at some point after the sharing of the peace and the passing of the offering plates before they handle the bread.

As has been so frequently observed, the cultures of local congregations differ, and so it is not surprising that practices of serving the meal will differ from place to place, even when options are offered. Some offer gluten-free bread as an option, or use it exclusively, as at Upper Room Fellowship. None of the congregations studied for this book reported the use of a pouring chalice, which is quite frequently used in Lutheran churches, but a pouring chalice preserves the virtues of both the common cup and the individual cup at the same time. The communicant takes an empty cup from a tray, and a server uses the chalice specially designed for pouring to fill it. It is possible to use either the typical glass or plastic cups so familiar to Presbyterians, or somewhat larger paper cups. The actual act of drinking has something to commend it.

Another issue likely to surface has to do with preparation. In churches that follow the typical practice of passing the elements in the pews, the most common practice is that someone cuts bread into small pieces and fills individual cups with grape juice (or sometimes cups of grape juice and also cups of wine). This requires fidelity to the task and a certain amount of time no matter the size of the congregation, but it is much more difficult in a large congregation.

When Moderator Neal Presa and the Session at Middlesex Presbyterian Church, a small congregation, decided to merge their 8:00 a.m. and 10:30 a.m. services, one issue was what to do about weekly Communion,

Problems, Obstacles, and Opportunities

which was the practice at 8:00 but not 10:30. Weekly Communion was important to the people accustomed to it at the 8:00 a.m. service. The Session was already trying to implement the proposals made in the *Invitation to Christ* document, and so were quite ready to agree to celebrate the meal in the new, single service every Sunday. The question was not whether they should do it, but how they should do it, and particularly, who would be responsible for preparation? The deacons agreed to provide the bread and fill the individual cups two Sundays a month. Neal and his wife, Grace, volunteered to do it the other two Sundays, and would also fill in if necessary if the assigned deacons had to be absent.

Pine Street Presbyterian Church in Harrisburg is a much larger congregation. When Fred Anderson began his pastorate there, he recalls receiving a phone call on the Saturday before his first Communion service telling him that they expected him to be available early on Sunday morning to cut the bread into cubes, "as only the pastor could do that."[8] Toward the end of Anderson's first year in Harrisburg, he brought up the issue of increasing the frequency of Communion for discussion in the Worship Committee. Many pastors will be aware that often the Worship Committee is organized for and mainly interested in taking care of practical details: flowers, ushers, Communion preparation and cleanup; and its members have been chosen because they have gifts to bring to the hands-on work of the committee. Because they are experienced with the various challenges posed by these practical tasks, it is not surprising when they are less interested in the theological, biblical, and historical issues than in the simple question, who will do it? This was true at Pine Street.

"How could we possibly do that every Sunday? Who would fill all those little cups every week? Did I really expect the women who prepared communion to give up every Saturday morning or afternoon to doing that? The woman who headed that group—a task she valued deeply and did with great devotion—was clear that this would be the end of her better than twenty years of service in that capacity," Anderson recalls.[9] When Anderson floated suggestions for possible solutions to the problem, he met resistance and decided to retreat and consider a different way to raise the question rather than beginning with the Worship Committee.

---

8. Ibid., part 1, 5.
9. Ibid., part 2, 2.

Working Out Solutions

At Pine Street, as the frequency of the Lord's Supper increased, the congregation experimented with various solutions to the problem of preparation and cleanup, as well as with ways to reduce the ceremonial comings and goings of the servers that is familiar to most Presbyterians and that takes so much time. At the 11:00 a.m. service, at which the bread and cup were distributed by passing them in the pews, the problem was resolved by delegating the task of cutting the bread and filling the cups to a member of the kitchen staff. Later, a different approach was taken: families were organized to bake or purchase the bread, prepare it, then fill the cups and set the Table on Sunday morning. The difficult task of washing individual glass cups at sufficient temperatures for maximum sanitary effectiveness was solved by giving up the glass cups and substituting plastic, a resolution embraced with awareness of ecological issues but resorted to nevertheless because it both lightened the heavy trays being passed in the pews and voided concerns about washing glasses to be reused. At the 8:30 service, the congregation comes forward to be served: first one is given the bread, then a filled plastic cup, which, after use, is placed in a basket and easily disposed of. At 11:00, where the people are served in the pews, the used cups are easily retrieved by deacons or family teams for disposal.

To reduce the time required to serve, the Session members at Pine Street availed themselves of the provision in the *Directory for Worship* that permits the use of deacons as servers. (It is also possible for the Session to commission any member to help serve.)[10] Given the sufficient number of church officers, one group of servers took the bread to the congregation, followed immediately by another group with trays of cups, and the people ate and drank as they were served. This shortened the time of communing by eight to ten minutes.

At Madison Avenue Church, where the meal is only rarely served in the pews, it has proven relatively easy to prepare for up to eight hundred people when they come forward to receive the bread and either dip it in the cup for intinction or drink from a common cup. Preparation takes twenty minutes or less, and can be accomplished by one person, whose duties include preparing two trays of bread and two of individual cups for those persons who cannot come forward and need to be served in the pew. It is, of course, important to make provision for persons who are not able to come

---

10. *DW*, W-3616d.

forward easily, and to be sure that someone is appointed to notice them and see to it that servers are alerted to take the bread and cup to serve them.

Whether celebrating the Lord's Supper weekly or less frequently, the challenge is to find a way to change the tone of the service so that the meal no longer resembles a memorial service for a dead Jesus but rather a meeting with the Lord who was crucified, but is risen. As Martha Moore-Keish has pointed out in her study of Presbyterian practice, that is hard to do even when the presiding minister follows the guidelines of the *Directory for Worship* and uses prayer texts directly from the *Book of Common Worship*. Moore-Keish describes the experience of a congregation in which she worshiped. Their custom was to celebrate the Lord's Supper once a month, using liturgical texts that accented joy and inclusiveness. Nevertheless, the tone of the service leaned toward the somber and the quiet. The congregation remained in their places, passing the bread and cup in the pews. Both movement and eye contact were minimal. The traditional way of doing things trumped the way the liturgical texts attempted to lift up the meal as joyful feast.

But then came a building project, a major renovation of the worship space, making it necessary to find an alternative meeting place on Sunday mornings. A neighboring Roman Catholic church offered them refuge. The change in venue required a shift in the way the congregation actually performed the Sacrament. The congregation began leaving their seats to process down the aisles to receive the bread and cup from servers at the front of the sanctuary. "Suddenly the mood was different. People looked at one another. They smiled. The servers and the partakers exchanged words over the bread and cup—something that had rarely happened before. The gathering took on the tone of a joyful celebration rather than of a sober time of individual reflection. This was not due to the words, which had hardly changed from one location to the other. But the assembly met God in a new way in that celebration, which changed their relationship to the Eucharist ever after."[11] A memorial meal had become a "jubilant feast," not based on new information but on new experience.

Elizabeth Deibert of Peace Presbyterian Church notes that in the church she serves, at first "there were quite a few long-time Presbyterians who really grieved" the loss of the experience of communing while seated in the pew. For their sake, the original plan had been to commune in the pews on occasion, but the desire for it "went away." She believes that "95

---

11. Moore-Keish, *Do This*, 72.

percent of the congregation would say they valued the participatory feeling of coming to the Table, and the community feeling of gathering." Again, experience spoke more loudly than reasoned explanations. Come and see.

For the congregation to move in procession toward the Table has the great virtue of enabling communicants to see each other's faces, and not just the backs of heads. Whatever diversity there may be in any particular congregation becomes visible when we move. We can see children, and the faces of parents with their children; we can see older people, sometimes moving carefully; we can see those who need a steadying hand on the elbow or to have a hand held. We can see people who look like us and people who don't, which is some sort of reminder that people will come "from east and west, from north and south, and will eat in the kingdom of God" (Luke 13:29). Processions require some kind of commitment, and they are festive by their very nature, and a procession to communion resembles our pilgrimage toward the new heaven and earth that God is fashioning for us.

Shifting the Dominant Mood

Even if processing for Communion is used only occasionally, it can, if carefully planned, shift the dominant mood of the Lord's Supper in a positive way without requiring elaborate explanations or arguments in its favor. As with anything new, at first people will experience either delight or apprehension (or both) as they learn how to do it. By the second time, the apprehension will have diminished dramatically.

Of course there is more than one opportunity in a Communion service for some kind of procession. At the 8:45 weekly Eucharist at First Presbyterian Church in Lexington, Kentucky, there is often a Great Entrance, when designated church members process to the Table to set it. The first person places the cloth on the Table, and the next hands to the presiding minister the bread, another the chalices, yet another the flagon to be placed on the Table. Several of the churches studied bring the bread and wine forward to be presented at the Table at the conclusion of the offertory at least occasionally.

Since the way music accompanies the rite contributes significantly to the way the rite is perceived and experienced, the various ways of using music might be a good place to begin evaluation when approaching the issue of changing the tone of the Communion service. Of course, more is involved than simply ordering that one sort of music be replaced by

Problems, Obstacles, and Opportunities

another. A healthy working relationship between minister and primary church musician is crucial to the whole process. Some ministers know a lot about music and appreciate it, while others do not. Some musicians know a lot about the history, theology, and practice of the church's worship, while others do not. Even if the musician is a pianist who has been playing at the same church for forty years, and the new minister has been on board for two months or two years and was a music minor at university, and neither believes there is anything to be learned from the other, collaboration is necessary. Respect for the other is the first step.

Most musicians in our churches are part time, and may not be available for staff meetings during daytime working hours. It is important that the minister responsible for worship and the primary musician find a way to meet, consult, and plan together regularly, even if that is not possible every week. Each needs to be both a teacher and a learner, and very often, they will be learning together. A smaller number of churches are able to employ a full-time musician, and in that case weekly staff meetings and frequent consultations are more easily done.

Fred Anderson is particularly sympathetic to church musicians because he has been one himself, having served as Director of Music at the Protestant Chapel at Norton Air Force Base during his senior year in college; and at both Pine Street and Madison Avenue he has worked with full-time music staff. Brant Copeland, of First Church in Tallahassee, is fortunate to have a part-time musician who is on the music faculty of Florida State University, with whom he has worked for years. Copeland describes Michael Corzine as "a world-class organist who sees himself as a servant of liturgy, and never puts himself forward. The Word is proclaimed in music as well as from the pulpit." Such a positive working relationship is much to be desired, and not always experienced everywhere. To change the tone of the Lord's Supper from something to be observed to something to be celebrated requires that pastor and musician understand the nature of the Sacrament and work together in such a way that the music will serve it as feast rather than funeral.

When Fred Anderson began his ministry at Madison Avenue, he was shocked to discover that a complete silence was kept throughout the entire process of distributing the bread and cup in the pews. When he inquired about the practice, it was explained that silence was kept in order not to disturb people's private devotions. After careful questioning, it was discovered that the majority of the congregation was quite happy to leave the total silence behind, but no one had felt they dared say anything since it had seemed such an untouchable tradition. Thanks to John Weaver, the church musician, as well as the choir, choral music began to accompany the distribution of the bread and cup. Weaver was delighted to be able to make use of the many Communion anthems available. Ultimately, in order to give the choir time to commune, Madison Avenue added congregational singing during the communion, using pieces from the ecumenical Taizé community in France. Silence throughout the entire communion service is too much, but silence does have a place: perhaps when all, or nearly all, have been served. At that point, a minute or two of silence adds one more dimension to the communal nature of the sacramental action.

Musical pieces from Taizé, a community founded originally by a Swiss Reformed pastor, are what musician Michael Hawn has described as "cyclical" music.[12] Cyclical music is just that—different from a hymn in that it recycles a relatively short piece of music over either a few or many repetitions. Both words and music can be learned easily after being heard once or twice, so that no printed text is necessary. Cyclical music can be sung by a congregation easily either with or without instrumental accompaniment. Many cyclical pieces can be sung very simply by the congregation (or choir) alone, or more elegantly with variations by adding a solo voice or instrumental accompaniment sung or played over the congregation's singing. Hawn identifies cyclical music as a perfect match for the performance of a rite. Hymns, with their more lengthy textual expositions, serve well to precede a rite or follow it. Several of the congregations studied make use of cyclical music while the people go forward to commune.

At Edgewood in Birmingham, a piece from Taizé, such as "Eat This Bread, Drink This Cup" is frequently sung.[13] When singing stops, the organist plays pieces in keeping with a celebration. At First Church in Owensboro, first the choir and then the congregation sing, as at Madison Avenue. At Lake Travis the congregation frequently sings "Come and fill our hearts with your peace" as they move toward the Table to commune, while Peace Church and First Church in Tallahassee often use similar pieces from Taizé also, although First Church is large enough that a sufficient number of people are in their places either before or after communing to sustain the singing of hymns as others commune. Peace Church makes use of rhythmic, upbeat music, especially during Easter and in Ordinary Time. Elizabeth

12. Hawn, *Gather*, 224ff.
13. GIA Publications, Chicago.

Problems, Obstacles, and Opportunities

Deibert says, "We might sing something that's very lively, for example, calypso, so that people are almost dancing as they prepare to approach the Table." If your congregation has an appetite for contemporary praise music, no doubt some of those pieces would serve the purpose.

At West Plano, they are fortunate to have in their midst Hal Hopson, widely known Presbyterian musician and composer, and they like to sing pieces he has written specifically for use as people approach the Table and receive the bread and cup.[14] The people sing during communion at Upper Room Fellowship in Pittsburgh and at Covenant Community in Louisville. Jud Hendrix of Covenant Community describes it as usually "up," energetic music, and adds that members of the congregation have written Communion songs, some of which the people sing together as they commune.

The Hot Metal Bridge Faith Community in Pittsburgh has a number of musicians in its midst. "Every week we have a different group that plays the music, because we want to get as many people involved as we possibly can. So, they'll usually pull together some music, and each week the music will be very, very different. It could be folk-punk, or it could be rhythm- or drum-centered, or it could have a reggae feel or a country feel or a rock feel. It mirrors who we are as a community, because everybody in the room is very, very different," says Jim Walker, one of the co-pastors.

Another very simple option as people process to receive the bread and cup is for the congregation to sing the likely familiar, simple setting of the single word *alleluia* to the hymn tune called Sinclair.[15] It is possible in the second time through the melody to substitute "Bread of heaven" in place of "Alleluia." For the third time through, the phrase "Cup of blessing" fits as well.

Adding the People's Voices

Presbyterian hymnals as well as those of other denominations include sung settings for those parts of the Great Thanksgiving ordinarily sung (or said) by the people, such as the Sanctus ("Holy, Holy, Holy Lord, God of power and might . . ."), the Memorial Acclamation ("Christ has died, Christ has risen, Christ will come again," or alternative texts; and the people's Great Amen at the end of the prayer, preceding the Lord's Prayer. A number of settings for these texts, in a variety of styles, are also available in a Presbyterian

---

14. Hopson, *Communion Songs*.
15. One source for this setting is Christian Reformed Church, *Psalter Hymnal*, #640.

publication called *Holy Is the Lord*.[16] When a congregation sings these consistently over a period of time, they can sing them as easily as "Praise God from Whom All Blessings Flow" or the Gloria Patri.

Holy Is the Lord includes an option for the presiding minister to sing part of the Great Thanksgiving with sung responses by the congregation, a practice followed not always but seasonally in Tallahassee. At Lake Travis, they often sing the Sanctus in Spanish—"Santo, Santo, Santo"—since Spanish is very much part of the Austin, Texas, cultural environment. At Edgewood, they sing one of the settings of the Lord's Prayer found in *The Presbyterian Hymnal*.

Sung responses engage the congregation in the flow of the eucharistic prayer and can help the people to discern its Trinitarian form. In addition to the three traditionally sung pieces of the Great Thanksgiving, consider adding a brief sung response after the petition (the epiclesis) that asks God to "pour out your Holy Spirit upon us and upon these your gifts of bread and wine . . ."[17] Again, the Taizé community offers several possibilities, including the simple chant "Holy Spirit, Come to Us." Reformed sacramental theology is dependent on the Holy Spirit. To reinforce the connections among them, the same sung piece might also be used after the petition for the Holy Spirit in the baptismal Thanksgiving over the Water, and again after the Prayer for Illumination preceding the reading of Scripture and the sermon. Using the same sung prayer for the Spirit in these three positions during a service helps to lift up the role of the Spirit in sacraments as well as in the sacramental character of Scripture reading and preaching.

Turning toward God's Ultimate Future

Problems and obstacles may be expected around any question that matters, but problems and obstacles are also opportunities. Presbyterian/Reformed practice is meant to be biblical, but we have been selectively biblical, resting our practice of the Lord's Supper very heavily on the *Last* Supper, with very little attention to other meal traditions recorded in both the Old and New Testaments. If we mean to be true to our frequently cited profession to be a church that is both reformed and *being* reformed *secundum verbi dei*, (i.e., "according to the word of God"), then the opportunity before us is to embrace a more expansive attention to the biblical meal traditions. Our

16. *Holy Is the Lord*.
17. *BCW*, 72.

Directory for Worship has already drawn our attention to these varied traditions. For example the *Directory* reads, "The New Testament describes the meal as a participation in Christ and with one another in the expectation of the Kingdom and as a foretaste of the messianic banquet."[18] The New Testament provides several examples of banquets understood as representations of the reign of God, and in the Gospel according to Luke, Jesus says, "Then people will come from east and west, from north and south, and will eat in the kingdom of God" (Luke 13:29), and Revelation includes the line, "Write this: Blessed are those who are invited to the marriage supper of the Lamb" (Rev 19:9).

Presbyterian practice of the Lord's Supper has tended to turn toward the past, with scant attention to the present, and even less to our hope for the kingdom, the new creation promised in the resurrection of the Lord. Although it is strongly present in the liturgical texts provided for the Great Thanksgivings in the *Book of Common Worship*, the eschatological promise (i.e., the promise that God's justice and mercy will have the last word in the form of the kingdom) is seldom represented in teaching or preaching, probably because we have tacitly chosen to leave those things to fundamentalists. It is, of course, challenging to deal with matters that can so easily be distorted and misused, but if we do not deal with them, we cut the Christian hope of a new heaven and earth down to a very small sort of hope indeed, and our claim to being biblical loses credibility.

These are bigger issues than the scope of this book allows, but our specific interest in the critique and reform of our eucharistic practice overlaps with eschatological issues in what at first seems like a very small question: Wine? Or grape juice? At Lake Travis Church, in Austin, both wine and grape juice are offered, as is the practice also in Harrison, Arkansas; Madison Avenue; and South Salem, New York. It would seem that nothing much is at stake here, since the idea is that the fruit of the vine is meant to represent the blood of Jesus, and either wine or grape juice would seem to have some sort of resemblance—both probably red, at least. But the use of wine in the Sacrament, whether a red wine or not, is much more than simply a representation of blood, since the New Testament language about eating and drinking Christ's flesh and blood is not about biological substances but about the person of Jesus himself. Wine, in both the Old and New Testaments, in part because it is a convivial drink, serves as an eschatological symbol—i.e., a symbol of the joy of God's kingdom.

---

18. W-2.4002.

Come and See

Amos 9:13, 14	John 2:10, 11
The time is surely coming, says the Lord . . . the mountains shall drip sweet wine, and all the hills shall flow with it . . . they shall plow vineyards and drink their wine . . .	"Everyone serves the good wine first . . . But you have kept the good wine until now." Jesus did this, the first of his signs, in Cana of Galilee, and revealed his glory.

Wine can be abused, as the Bible itself contends, but it is different from both water and grape juice in that its purpose is more than a utilitarian quenching of thirst. Wine is the drink of conviviality, a drink of celebration. The miracle at the wedding in Cana, a difficult text for preachers, is not about Jesus coming to the rescue of his embarrassed host. Turning water used for Jewish religious ceremonies into an abundance of wine, the first of the signs revealing his glory, signals that in Jesus, the joyful kingdom that is to come is being made manifest right then, in him and in his ministry. Jesus is bread "to strengthen the human heart" and he is also "wine to gladden the human heart" (Ps 104:15). The sacred meal is meant to be a foretaste of the joy of the kingdom. Wine, then, is in every way quite different from grape juice, both because it represents gladness and because it represents the kingdom that both has been and will be made manifest in Christ. Grape juice represents neither.

Presbyterians were not as eager as Methodists to adopt the results of the newly invented chemistry of preventing the fermentation of the grape, the brainchild of Mr. Welch, a Methodist layman. Unfermented grape juice was not approved by the General Assemblies of either the Northern or Southern Presbyterian Churches until after the turn of the twentieth century. (The Southern church resisted longer than the Northern.) But both finally gave in, swept along by the temperance movement of the era, which was really a teetotaling movement, rooted not only in opposition to alcohol abuse but also in suspicion of new immigrants and their customs. After more than a hundred years, grape juice seems to us to be the normal contents of the communion cup, in spite of two millennia of using wine as the sacramental drink for the greater number of Christians in the world, including most Reformed.

Fred Anderson recalls that wine was too great a step for the Pine Street congregation, who might drink wine at home but felt that, somehow, wine had no place in the church building. And then, of course there is the often-raised fear that wine might put too great a temptation in the path of recovering alcoholics. Certainly this fear is to be taken seriously. Indeed, both wine and grape juice had best be offered. In situations where grape juice is not available, recovering alcoholics are welcome to take the Communion bread alone and in so doing are truly united with Christ, receiving a full measure of God's healing grace. Wine, like any other material, can be abused and so is potentially dangerous. But for many, wine provides a taste of the festive drink that anticipates the joy of the kingdom. Drinking wine is thus an entirely different experience from drinking grape juice.

Does that mean that there is no real Sacrament unless wine is used? No. The Holy Spirit is not dependent on us to get it all absolutely right, even if we were completely certain about what that would be. The Holy Spirit could work even amid the distortions of the medieval Mass as well as in the exaggerations and reductions of hard-line Puritanism, and can work when we hardly know what we are doing and simply stumble through the best we know how. We are not eager to put obstacles in the Spirit's way, though, challenging God by deliberate indifference or carelessness. But pastoral issues matter, and congregations need to do the best they can, putting first things first. If wine seems too big a stretch, then let it be grape juice. The *Directory for Worship* states, "Whenever wine is used in the Lord's Supper, unfermented grape juice should always be clearly identified and served also as an alternative for those who prefer it."[19] It might be a matter of wisdom to add another line: "Whenever grape juice is used, wine should always be clearly identified and served also as an alternative for those who prefer it."

When I was serving as pastor of a congregation in Lexington, Kentucky, the chair of the Worship Committee initiated a move to return to the use of wine in the Lord's Supper, while providing grape juice as an alternative. Her motion passed the Session unanimously, and was instituted without a single murmur from the congregation, and it remains the practice after twenty-five years. In fact, a discussion of the differences between wine and grape juice might be just the right starting point to initiate a profound discussion about what the Lord's Supper actually is meant to be—one best undertaken in a meeting when there is no motion in play.

---

19. W-3.3611.

Four

Introducing Change Successfully

Leadership

More Presbyterian ministers serving as pastors of congregations believe in weekly Communion than serve congregations that actually practice it. Maybe they are waiting, whether consciously or not, for someone else to make it happen. Maybe the General Assembly, or the local presbytery, will strongly urge congregations to establish a goal of working toward weekly celebration of the Lord's Supper, and Sessions that are inclined to respect denominational initiatives will rise to the challenge without the pastor having to lead the way. Or maybe within their pastoral lifetimes a critical mass of Presbyterian congregations will become weekly-Eucharist churches, and other congregations will follow their example, with pastors needing only to go with the flow rather than to make the first move. If one were to place a wager, the last possibility is a stronger likelihood than the others, but only if pastors somewhere, somehow, take the initiative that may lead, eventually, to the necessary critical mass. Who will those pastors be?

Ministers newly called to a pastorate have been cautioned not to make changes too fast. Let the congregation learn to know and at least begin to develop some trust in their new pastor, the counsel goes. Let the new pastor start out as a respectful learner, getting to know members of the church and how the congregation works and who makes it work and where the land mines are and where to find the points of leverage. Then, when the introductory period is past, consider what sort of leadership moves might be required to strengthen the congregation and its ministry. So goes the prevailing wisdom.

Of course, a risk in moving slowly is that the pastor will settle in so well that it seems easier simply to adapt to the ways of the congregation without stirring anything up with any suggestion of change. After all, the people who are already there, and who stay there, are likely to be those who are either satisfied with things as they are or at least making the best of it. They are the ones who are willing to serve as church officers or committee members or teachers, and they are the ones who pay the bills. Why risk troubling the waters? Especially, why take a risk on behalf of people who are not there, and not paying the bills, and who may never be there?

On the other hand, some question the ubiquitous but mostly unwritten rule that warns the new pastor to take it slowly. After all, one of the assets the new pastor brings to the congregation is a fresh eye. The newcomer notices not only what is there, but also what is not there; not only who is there, but who might be there; not only what is being done, but what might be done. The freshness of the newcomer's assessment of what might be and could be diminishes quickly enough as the new pastor becomes assimilated, having moved from outsider to insider.

No doubt there is a strong case to be made for moving slowly and perhaps also one for moving more quickly, and we will take a look at both, beginning with the older tradition of starting slowly. Whether later or sooner, however, the question remains, why stir up the waters? The answer is always the same: challenging the status quo is what leadership is about. Not stirring up trouble but actually leading—seeing what might be, and doing one's best to share the vision and working with others to discover how to realize it. Pastors need to lead; certainly that is not in dispute. The only question is how to do that effectively, and that requires assessing the congregational culture and trying out some strategies to see how they go.

Perhaps your pastor has had the experience some others have had: receiving a Church Information Form (CIF) prepared by a congregation in search of a new pastor. The CIF identifies the challenges of the congregation: we are aging, our numbers are decreasing, pledges are not keeping up with the budget, the neighborhood is changing. And then, the CIF declares, whether directly or indirectly, "We need a pastor who can help us grow again—but without changing anything." Few are likely to accept a call on those terms, but if it should happen, the pastor cannot escape the responsibility of discerning what the possibilities are and working with the congregation to help them to imagine new possibilities as well, and to embrace or at least consent to the change that inevitably proves necessary. This may be done very carefully, very gently, but it will have to be done if the pastor is actually to be faithful to the God who calls both pastor and people, however reluctant both may be to hazard the risks at stake in responding to that call.

Leadership requires taking risks, but it need not be foolhardy. Fred Anderson, who led two congregations to weekly Eucharist, writes "I had come to learn that asking a 'What if . . . ?' question was a far less threatening way to introduce the possibility of change than simply saying, 'Let's try it this way.'"[1] It is far easier to introduce a topic for discussion than to lay out an agenda.

Change Takes Time

The year before Anderson became pastor of Pine Street Presbyterian Church in Harrisburg in 1980, the congregation of about a thousand members had begun celebrating the Lord's Supper bimonthly in place of quarterly. Near the end of Anderson's first year in Harrisburg, he approached the Worship Committee and broached the idea of weekly Communion, the use of a common cup, and the introduction of wine: he immediately discovered that he had started the conversation at the wrong place and the wrong time. Retreating, he waited for five years.

The next time, Anderson began to address the issue of weekly Communion in sermons, usually on Sundays when the Supper was celebrated. Feedback from the congregation made it apparent that he had piqued people's interest. To encourage conversation, he scheduled a few occasions in which people were invited to respond to the sermon and discuss the issues raised.

An elder asked Anderson how to go about getting the question of weekly Communion before the Session. Anderson encouraged him to bring his concern to a Session meeting, and he did, stimulating a lively discussion. The Session asked their pastor to bring to subsequent meetings a series of presentations on the history and theology of the Lord's Supper, and these aroused even more interest, resulting in a commitment to set aside time for the Session to study relevant biblical texts. The texts were announced before the meeting, giving the elders time to read and reflect

1. Anderson, "Toward Every Sunday," part 4, 17, n.19

on them and to formulate their questions. At Session meetings the elders spent thirty or forty minutes in study and discussion. They also consented to read Calvin's *Institutes* on worship, as well as his "Treatise on the Lord's Supper" and several publications produced by the General Assembly's Office of Worship.

The Session asked the Worship Committee to begin their own discussions, requesting that they take care to note their concerns as well as the concerns of members of the congregation. Further, the Session wanted to begin to widen the conversation in the congregation as a whole. The wider discussion began with Pine Street's annual Intergenerational Winter Seminar, which the planners chose to devote to a discussion of the Sacraments. This topic aroused so much interest that the Session urged that it be continued the following year, this time focused specifically on the Lord's Supper. Pine Street Church had seven or eight adult classes that met on Sunday mornings, and they began to pick up on the conversation as well. The church's newsletter reported on the studies, and Anderson wrote articles on specific topics related to the Lord's Supper.

The Pine Street Session decided to increase the frequency of the Lord's Supper from bimonthly to monthly. Ample time had been spent dealing with historical and theological issues, but now it became time to address logistics. The church body was accustomed to having only elders serve the people. The question was whether they needed to increase the size of the Session again, as they had earlier when going from quarterly to bimonthly celebrations. Anderson reminded them that not only did the *Directory for Worship* permit deacons to serve, but that the office of deacon had been created in the first place, according to the book of Acts, to assist with the serving of tables. This provided an easy solution to the need for more personnel to serve a more frequent traditional pew Communion. Other logistical questions had to do with how to shorten the ceremonial comings and goings of the servers in a traditional Presbyterian Communion service, and of course, with a bit of experimentation, satisfactory ways were found for solving those difficulties, reducing the usual time needed for the action at the Table and communion of the people by ten to fifteen minutes.

Anderson and the Session invited feedback from the congregation. Anderson believes that it is important to tell the congregation what is being done and why rather than to surprise them. And, he suggests, "Let them know that this is not 'forever' and can be changed whenever, if need be.

Set a deadline for evaluation, and let them know what decisions have been made."[2]

The Session voted on the question: "Should we begin celebrating the Lord's Supper weekly?" It was stated this way intentionally, as a policy question, not as a decision to adopt the practice immediately. An affirmative vote would be a commitment to begin exploration of how it might be done. Anderson asked that the ballot be secret so that elders would be completely free to vote their own consciences without feeling either peer pressure or a need to please the moderator. The vote was fourteen yeses to three noes, with one abstention. Session appointed a task force, to be chaired by its clerk, to study implementation of the motion. The clerk was a supporter of weekly Communion, but the task force also included the three members who had most probably cast the *no* votes and the elder who identified himself as the abstaining vote, along with the elder who had originally raised the question, and the chair of the Worship Committee. The task force as constituted thus included three who had voted in favor of the motion, three who had opposed it, and one who had abstained. The mandate to the task force was to bring a recommendation to the Session, but only when they were all in agreement. They were given up to five years to do their work.

The task force met monthly for the next three years. Their first recommendation was to add the Lord's Supper on Christmas Eve, Easter Day, and Pentecost to the regular first-Sunday celebrations and annual Maundy Thursday Communion. Within a year they recommended adding the First Sunday in Advent, Epiphany, Baptism of the Lord, Transfiguration, First Sunday in Lent, Trinity Sunday, and Christ the King Sunday. Depending on when these fell, the congregation often found that the meal was being celebrated two or even three Sundays in a row.

The 8:30 congregation wanted the Lord's Supper to be celebrated every week, the task force recommended it, and the Session approved it. For the summer, the two services combined, and the people who worshiped at 8:30 made it clear that they wanted weekly Communion at the single summer service, and Session agreed. At a called meeting of the Session the first week of September, and based on the congregation's positive experience during the summer, Session decided unanimously to celebrate the Lord's Supper every week in both services from then on.

Even with this very careful and unhurried planning with every opportunity for discussion and feedback, and bending over backwards not to

2. Ibid., part 2, 6.

stack the decks when decisions were to be made, it is not surprising that not everyone welcomed weekly Communion. A few people "not only chose not to commune, but drew attention to the point by folding their arms when the servers came to them."[3] Their friends reminded them that they could at least pass the elements even if they chose not to participate.

Anderson felt the process was complete when he heard one of the members who had been so resistant to all this tell a visitor, "Yes, we observe the Lord's Supper weekly; it is a very important part of our worship and one of the things that sets us apart from any other Presbyterian church in this town."[4]

Will It Outlast the Present Pastorate?

Of course, the real test for any change that has been instituted during a pastorate is what happens when the pastor leaves. A pastor who served a Presbyterian congregation in Oregon had advocated for weekly Communion, and in the second year of his pastorate the Session agreed to the practice, which was framed as something to be tried for a calendar year. They also worked out the logistics related to more frequent preparation, the length of the service, and the like, and began to practice weekly Eucharist, with pew Communion on the first Sunday of the month. On the other Sundays the congregation came forward to commune by intinction. The trial year was up at the end of December, but the congregation continued weekly Communion only through January, after which the pastor, who had been engaged to a woman who was also a minister, left to marry. At that point, the congregation returned to celebrating Communion once a month. In retrospect, the pastor has come to believe that although the congregation was ready to trust him and follow his lead, they had not been adequately prepared for weekly Eucharist and took no real ownership of the practice. When it became necessary to fill the pulpit week by week after he left (they did not have an interim), the congregation simply gave it up.

The case at Pine Street was quite different. When Anderson left, a prominent member and teacher of an adult class wrote a letter to the Session and to the Mission Review Committee urging that they discontinue weekly Communion now that the pastor who had so strongly championed the practice was gone. Both the Session and the Mission Review Committee

3. Ibid., part 2, 11.
4. Ibid., part 2, 12.

responded that "weekly communion had become central to the spiritual nurture of the congregation as well as an important part of the congregation's identity."[5] Weekly Eucharist is still the practice at Pine Street after more than twenty years.

Patience

Not being in too big a hurry can work wonders. From my own pastoral experience, however, I can say that it is far easier to take the short view than the long view. What undertakings are most likely to produce a victory or two sooner in a pastorate rather than later? Getting some project conceived, launched, and celebrated raises the morale of the congregation while making the next success come a little easier. Like others who take their work seriously, the pastor feels the satisfaction of being able to identify a list of tangible contributions to the life of the church. And yet, in retrospect, it is easy to see that some worthy projects require a longer horizon—perhaps not always coming to fruition even during the present pastorate. Alongside pursuing those changes that are more quickly realized, there is virtue in taking the long view in some instances, and that requires patience.

Brant Copeland is a patient man, and he has had to be. He became pastor of First Presbyterian Church in Tallahassee in 1985. First Church is not far from the Florida state capitol, and it is not unusual for governors to walk by the church on their way to work. The church is known for prophetic preaching, and as a congregation has been inclined to take progressive views on issues of social justice. Members are highly educated, most working in education, government, or social services.

As I noted earlier, Brant Copeland, a child of a Southern Church manse, had experienced something of a sacramental conversion experience when he was a student in a Scottish university before enrolling at Union Seminary in Richmond. That eye-opening experience was not one to be enjoyed only privately, but one that awakened him to possibilities that he has felt led to share, and Copeland has devoted a good deal of his ministry to encouraging and even urging Presbyterians to rediscover the Eucharist as a meeting with the risen Lord. He is persuaded that the Lord's Supper is normative for Lord's Day worship.

Copeland made clear to his congregation in both teaching and preaching that it was his dream that weekly Eucharist might become the norm at

---

5. Ibid., part 2, 13.

First Presbyterian Church. The congregation's worship has become more profoundly biblical and Presbyterian, recovering the singing of Psalms and making use of the rich texts of Great Thanksgivings in the *Book of Common Worship*. Pew communion is occasional, replaced most of the time by the congregation's coming forward to commune at the Table. Over time, the frequency of Communion increased, first from about once every six weeks, as it was at the beginning of Copeland's pastorate, to once a month. And then, in the spring of 1998, an elder was ready to propose to the Session that the congregation begin a weekly celebration of the meal beginning in the fall.

Copeland wanted to proceed as carefully as possible in order that this move be one for which both Session and congregation could genuinely take ownership rather than one taken to please himself, so he made an alternate proposal. His suggestion was that the Session commit to a year for study and discernment, using the time for the congregation to reflect on this proposed change, and the Session agreed. In the year following, both pros and cons were carefully considered, and strong feelings were exposed on both sides. Church members who opposed the move gathered signatures on a letter opposing weekly celebration, while others wrote of their approval.

At the end of the discernment year, in the spring of 1999, the Session voted to begin the practice of weekly Communion in the fall for a period of fifteen months, concluding at the end of the year 2000. Over the course of the fifteen months, many members welcomed weekly Communion with appreciation, and some who had originally been opposed reported that the experience had caused them to change their minds. Many parents of young children were particularly pleased with weekly celebration.

As the date approached for making a permanent commitment to weekly Communion, the Session held open meetings and received more letters, both for and against. Some of the letters in opposition were clearly deeply felt, and they tended to represent the most familiar objections. Weekly Communion was too Catholic; it turned the meal into a "routine, mechanical ritual"; it wasted time that might better be spent on the sermon. While many of the letters approving of the practice were moving, one of them is particularly striking: "For the members of our family who cannot hear, who cannot see, the act of receiving the Sacraments is the only tactile way in which to experience worship. What a wonderful gift."[6]

---

6. Copeland, *Eucharist*, 18.

The Session, weighing not so much the numbers but the intensity of the opposition, decided that the prudent thing was to pull back, and they suspended weekly Communion. Instead, they adopted a schedule for celebrating the Lord's Supper on the first and third Sundays of every month, plus on the big Sundays in the liturgical calendar, such as Christmas Eve, Transfiguration, the Great Vigil of Easter, Easter Sunday and every Sunday during Eastertide, and on Pentecost—in 2013 a total of thirty-five out of fifty-two Sundays, plus at four evening services.

More than ten years has passed. Minds and hearts have been changed, and those who objected most strongly have, for the most part, either changed their minds or have passed on. A few have told Copeland that they don't know why they opposed weekly Communion back then. Within six months of the decision to pull back, two elders who were on the Session at the time of that decision approached their pastor as things began to settle down, saying, "I love it. I don't know why I was opposed to this. I can see what a difference it makes." Others have noted how the absence of the Sacrament is so noticeable on non-Communion Sundays. Children in particular feel the absence. And people ask, "Why don't we have weekly Communion?"

Copeland notes that there is no good answer to the question. He is tempted to find a way to have the question brought before the Session, and has no doubt that a motion to institute weekly Communion would pass now, but he is waiting for them to make the move rather than taking the initiative. Some members have been in the congregation long enough to remember a short earlier pastorate that was marked by conflict, and Copeland wanted to spare them a repeat of that unhappy experience. He did not want to realize his dream at the expense of pastoral effectiveness. He is waiting, practicing patience.

Act Two

Fred Anderson became pastor of Madison Avenue Presbyterian Church in March of 1992. Like the Pine Street congregation, Madison Avenue had a strong preaching tradition, including Anderson's immediate predecessor, David H. C. Read, as well as earlier pastors George Buttrick and Henry Sloane Coffin. After spending years introducing weekly Eucharist in Harrisburg, was Anderson really going to do it again in New York? Anderson's first commitment was to earn the trust of the congregation. There were many unrelated issues requiring attention early on, and it seemed to be prudent to keep the worship practices of the congregation as stable as possible.

At Madison Avenue, it is not unusual for many members to be out of town on a Sunday morning, and the Worship Committee was concerned about this as had been the Pastoral Nominating Committee. Starting a new service is ordinarily easier than introducing big changes in an existing one, since it requires no one to alter their existing pattern unless they choose to attend the new service. In September 1992, a service was started at 7:00 p.m. on Sunday evenings, and it included weekly Communion. Other than this new service, Anderson decided not to initiate any other changes in worship for at least a year.

During David H. C. Read's pastorate, he had introduced a Service for Healing and Wholeness, which had been discontinued when Read retired, but those who had attended it missed it. The Worship Committee agreed to offer it again on the first Wednesday of the month, in the chapel, beginning in October of 1993. This time, the service not only included the laying on of hands and prayers for those who chose to go forward, but also the Lord's Supper, which helped to lead everyone present to enter more deeply into the service.

At a Session retreat in the second year of Anderson's pastorate, the Lord's Supper was celebrated using a common cup of wine. One of the people who had been on the retreat suggested that wine and a common cup be introduced at the 9:30 a.m. service, at which people were already accustomed to coming to the Table in small groups on Communion Sundays. The Worship Committee and Session agreed, but added a chalice of grape juice to be used exclusively for Communion by intinction.

Even though those who are accustomed to grape juice at Communion sometimes object to wine so as to be considerate of those recovering from alcoholism, Anderson has found that it is worthwhile to discuss the issue with recovering alcoholics themselves. He writes, "I have found them to be most helpful and never wanting to limit the faith community's experience because of their own hardship. Many find the discipline of abstaining from the cup a strong reinforcement of their own commitments, and a grace that sustains them in and of itself . . . However they deal with the issue, have them be a part of the conversation in your decision making, if they are willing."[7]

---

7. Anderson, "Toward Every Sunday," part 4, 7.

In summertime, the Madison Avenue Church offers only a single service on Sunday mornings. The people attending at 9:30 had grown accustomed to coming forward for Communion, and to being able to choose a common cup and wine. How would they commune on Communion Sundays when two services merged into one for the summer? In June of 1994, the 9:30 practice was introduced at the combined summer service: a common cup of wine was offered (intinction was an option) as well as individual cups of grape juice.

Madison Avenue had not celebrated the Lord's Supper on Easter Sunday, but in 1994, Easter fell on a first Sunday, a Communion Sunday. They did not shrink from the challenge, but celebrated the meal on Easter, and have continued every Easter since.

The congregation was becoming accustomed to Communion in several settings, and had been introduced to more than one way of receiving the bread and cup. In the more than four years since Anderson began his pastorate there, he had not brought the question of weekly Communion to the Session, but a new elder, who had family in Harrisburg and had frequently visited Pine Street, became a member of the Worship Committee. She wanted to bring the issue of weekly Communion to the Session, and Anderson welcomed her leadership. In the year following, his sermons, especially on Communion Sundays, began to unfold new dimensions of the Lord's Supper and the benefits of weekly celebration.

The church had adjusted its schedule so that Christian Education and worship did not occur at the same hour, and Anderson took the opportunity to teach, offering a four-week course on Reformed worship, focusing on the unity of Word and Sacrament on the Lord's Day. As he engaged the class in discussion, it became apparent that for the congregation, the Lord's Supper was "private and largely penitential," more of "a memory and devotional exercise" than an encounter with the risen Lord. Anderson brought in liturgical scholars to teach, perhaps building on the observation that those who have to travel to make a presentation are somehow granted an authority not as readily granted to local people whose expertise is often considerable. The outside scholars effectively reinforced what Anderson had been teaching and advocating.

Early in 1999, acting on a motion from the Worship Committee, the Session voted to begin a time of discussion and education about weekly Communion, and they devoted thirty to forty-five minutes of each Session meeting to it. The next step seemed to be moving the question along by exposing people to the actual experience of more frequent Communion, so Session affirmed a motion from the Worship Committee to add festival days to the Communion calendar along with the first Sunday of each month. "The committee believed this was necessary if the congregation were ever to learn that, in this instance, familiarity does not breed contempt nor lessen the sacrament's meaning."[8] Come and see!

Change

Any change arouses a certain level of resistance, whether the change is a capital-funds campaign, the establishment of a peacemaking committee, a personnel change, a decision about outside groups using the building, a revision of the wedding policy, or a change in the Sunday service. Some members of Madison Avenue did not favor the increase in the frequency of celebration of the Sacrament, offering the same objections as were raised at Pine Street and Tallahassee. The objections were not so much theological as emotional. Differences of opinion should never come as a surprise. Our Presbyterian forebears created our Form of Government precisely because they believed that differences of opinion were to be expected. The question is how to deal with them, and answering that question requires pastoral sensitivity without expecting that it is a simple matter of the majority ruling, or, for that matter, of the minority having the last word.

Weekly Communion, like the capital campaign or the new wedding policy, or a controversial decision by the General Assembly, may result in the loss of some members. Leaders lead, and sometimes it requires choosing between a call to faithfulness and the relative comfort of preserving the status quo. The controversial decision that causes the loss of some members is likely also to draw some who otherwise might not have been drawn to the congregation, and to sustain some members who might under other circumstances have fallen away. The same change that threatens some deeply attracts others who were not there to be counted when the change was initiated.

At the Session meeting in February 2002, the chair of the Madison Avenue Worship Committee introduced a motion that "the session approve celebration of the Lord's Supper at each Lord's Day service, as well as all festival services, and that the worship committee develop a strategy

---

8. Ibid., part 3, 12.

for implementation of weekly communion within the next two years."[9] The motion carried, unanimously. After the leadership had listened to members of the congregation, the decision was made to commune in the pews four times a year. (In 2007, reviewing the practice of pew communion quarterly, Session decided to continue it only at Easter.) Madison Avenue began celebrating the Lord's Supper weekly in all its Lord's Day services on the first Sunday in February 2002, nine years and eleven months after Fred Anderson had become pastor. Patience.

On the Other Hand

Just as some persons will be the last to buy a smartphone and the last to learn how to use a computer, there are others who will be among the first to adopt new technologies. Presbyterian congregations all follow the same polity, and their officers answer the same constitutional questions when ordained and installed, but they are not all alike. Some congregations move slowly and carefully. Others might be described as early adopters. The same goes for Presbyterian ministers. Charles (Chip) Andrus offers this pastoral advice: "First, you have to get rid of the notion that as a new pastor you need to wait a year before you do anything. When I interviewed for my current call at South Salem Presbyterian in South Salem (Lewisboro), New York, I told the pastoral nominating committee right up front that I would be pushing them to move to weekly communion. They knew what they were getting into."[10]

Like Fred Anderson, Chip Andrus has introduced weekly Eucharist in two congregations. Andrus became pastor in Harrison, Arkansas, in November 2006. During the first Lenten season of his pastorate, classes were offered on "Living into Our Baptism." At the same time, the congregation was preparing to move into a new building. As they left the old building and entered the new one during Holy Week, with particular attention to the three days (Maundy Thursday, Good Friday, and Easter Vigil), the move proved to be a kind of dramatization of the congregation's experience of death and resurrection.

When Andrus became pastor, the congregation had two morning services, the early one meeting in the fellowship hall and styled as contemporary, but the people were getting tired of it. Andrus suggested weekly

---

9. Ibid., part 3, 13.
10. Andrus, "Moving to Weekly Eucharist," 36.

Communion in that service, beginning in Advent, only a month after he began his pastorate. The congregation of the early service not only loved Communion every week, but one of the attenders wondered aloud in a Session meeting whether the people who worshiped at 11:00 a.m. might be envious of them!

As soon as he had arrived, Andrus offered Morning Prayer at 8:30 a.m. on weekday mornings, Tuesday through Friday. The organist, who practiced at the church every day, was happy to play for Morning Prayer. The new pastor discovered teachable moments during which he could talk to the people about the rhythm of the day as related to the week, and about the week in relation to the liturgical year, and about worship centered on both the Word and the breaking of bread every Sunday, and about how the weekly breaking of bread distinguished Sunday as the Lord's Day. "Once people have become immersed in the practice of Daily Prayer, they begin to appreciate the stark contrast between the Service of the Word—which is the basic pattern of Daily Prayer—and a Service of Word and Sacrament—the fullness of the church's worship on the Lord's Day," Andrus observes.[11]

Andrus understood that the congregation's move into a new building offered a huge opportunity. He believed that weekly Communion would help the church to grow in all the important ways, not just numerically, but spiritually and in nourishing a sense of mission. A goal was to find and form a core of people to share this vision. He was intentional about getting into as many homes as possible, and also sought out teaching opportunities. Andrus is a musician and began to play in a blue-collar club once a week, which he discovered to be a good place for conversations about expanding the church's table to reach out to others.

Andrus held meetings in which to study the lectionary readings. He taught the faith by helping people to learn about and reflect on the actual movements of the Sunday liturgy. He spoke about why we do these things in the order we do them, and how each liturgical action relates to everyday life. In that setting, he found that by discussing liturgical practices, it was easy to identify and draw contrasts with the dominant cultural theologies represented in the larger Harrison community. Those discussions offered the opportunity to talk about weekly Eucharist, rehearsing the story of the two disciples whom Jesus met and taught on the Emmaus road. Andrus taught that it was important for us, as for those two, to invite Christ to the Table instead of letting him go on as though he were, in fact, no more than

---

11. Ibid., 37.

a stranger. He urged them to think of worship not just as something people do, but about "opening up space for the Spirit in our lives."

After a number of general and specific ways of preparing the congregation, including the Lenten studies, and anticipating the move into the new building, Andrus proposed to the Worship Committee that the Lord's Supper be celebrated weekly beginning Easter Sunday, in the new sanctuary, and continuing throughout the Sundays of Easter. The Session accepted the committee's recommendation. As Pentecost approached, the Worship Committee faced the prospect that without further Session action, the congregation would revert to its earlier practice of monthly Communion. They brought to the Session their recommendation that the congregation continue to celebrate the meal every week. The motion was not received as enthusiastically, but it passed without objection.

Some resistance emerged in response to the inauguration of weekly Communion. It came from members who had not attended any of the classes or participated in any of the preparation. The resisters actually staged a protest by walking out of the service during the singing of a doxology at the offering. Andrus immediately visited each of them in their homes, and the result was that they called off the protest and began staying for the whole service. At first, a few of the protesters opted not to come forward to receive the Sacrament, but by the end of his tenure, all were coming to the Table. By pastoral care he had managed either to win them over, or at least persuade them that weekly Eucharist had been undertaken for the good of the church.

Another Second Act

In 2011, Hudson River Presbytery appointed Andrus designated pastor of South Salem Presbyterian Church. The congregation had undergone a difficult period during the previous pastorate, which resulted in a large exodus. Andrus moved to South Salem in June, a month that usually marks a summertime decline in worship attendance, but by the end of summer 2011, attendance had risen to more than twice the number normally attending during the school year. Presbytery's committee had advised Andrus to be up-front with the congregation about his commitments, and he made it known to the committee and church members before he arrived that he intended to lead them to weekly Communion or, if not successful in that, to seek another call. It seemed clear to everyone that either the church would die under Andrus's tenure or bounce back, but there was no doubt that it was a do-or-die moment, and the congregation was ready to take some risks. A study of the congregation revealed that most wanted a "traditional" service rather than looking for solutions in technological innovations.

Andrus is creative in seeking out a variety of ways to get to know people and to engage them in conversation about matters of substance. The Northeastern culture is different from that of Harrison, Arkansas, and it soon became clear that pastoral calling, in the traditional sense, did not work as well in New York. People's schedules and those of their children had shaped a different set of expectations. Across the street from the church was a pub, and Andrus found that it served as an inviting place to meet people and get to know them.

The South Salem congregation had no adult-education program, and Sunday School had been held at the same time as worship: children up to sixth grade were dismissed from the service to go to their classes. Leadership decided to separate the times for education and worship. This gave Andrus the opportunity to begin a class (not identified as such). Bagels and coffee were provided in the church narthex. Andrus engaged the people in conversation about a favorite subject: the liturgy of the church and the ecology of every part of the liturgy. No part of it is dispensable since the whole of it—Word and Sacrament—form and shape the faith of the people.

With the support of the chair of the Worship Committee, the decision was made to begin the practice of weekly Communion on World Communion Sunday, the first Sunday in October. Clearly, it was important to use every opportunity throughout September to talk with the people about the upcoming change in practice. Classes were held on Wednesday nights and on Sundays after church; other discussions took place in casual settings.

Working with a colleague, Jonathan Carroll, Andrus had developed a course about the Sacraments. At the first meeting, Andrus set out a bowl of water, and initiated a conversation about water, including both biblical and personal stories about water. He asked those present to write prayers of thanksgiving for water, naming springs and lakes in the area. At the next meeting, he presented a loaf of bread that they broke and ate with butter and jam. This time, the stories were about bread—beginning once again with stories from the Bible, but including stories about the experiences of those present that had to do with bread. Finally they wrote prayers of thanksgiving for bread. The third week was the week for wine. That gathering followed the same format as the two earlier meetings had, and concluded with writing poems about wine. At the next gathering, they talked about words, and at the one after that, they reflected about time. For the last meeting, they watched the movie *Babette's Feast* and shared a meal that had been prepared for them.

When one class reached completion, Andrus offered another, and then others following the same pattern. The protocol was that once a class began, no new members were admitted so that those in the group could develop a sense of community that would not be risked by members' coming and going. People not in the class became curious about it, making it easy to form the next one, and Andrus discovered that those who had completed a class were eager to prepare the closing meal for the following group.

As one might expect, not everyone in the congregation understood or appreciated the move toward weekly Eucharist, raising the usual questions about losing something special, about the length of the service, and about preparation. But the resistance was minimal. Andrus reports that "the congregation . . . moved to weekly communion after three months of education and intentional conversations about the importance of reclaiming a full service of Word and Sacrament weekly."[12]

The people of the congregation go forward to commune, using either a common cup of wine or, for intinction, one with grape juice, as well as a tray of individual cups with either wine or grape juice. Members of the community bake the bread and are eager to have a turn doing it. A member of the community has donated the wine. Servers place bread in the people's hands—a new practice vigorously advocated now by elders and other members.

A few vocal members would not come to any of the educational offerings, but eventually all but two gave up their objections. If an objection should arise, Andrus finds that it is not necessary for him to be the one who responds, because others speak up for their new way of celebrating the meal, and celebrating it every week.

South Salem's sanctuary faces toward the church's historic graveyard, and at the rear of the chancel is a huge window providing a panoramic view of the gravestones. On the Communion Table, constructed from wood rescued from a church fire that destroyed the building in 1973, is inscribed "I am the Bread of Life." As the congregation is led in the eucharistic prayer every Sunday, looking both toward the Table and beyond it to the graveyard,

---

12. Andrus, "Moving toward Weekly Eucharist," 38.

the reverent evocation of "choirs of angels" and "the faithful of every time and place" is especially vivid.

Not Long, Not Short

When Jonathan Carroll became pastor of First Presbyterian Church in Owensboro, Kentucky, he resolved not to introduce any changes in the congregation's worship in the first year and a half. Then he began conversations about how the church might utilize the font and Table more purposefully. When the 217th General Assembly approved the document *Invitation to Christ*, Carroll felt as though he had the support of the denomination to encourage exploration following its recommendations. The Session began a yearlong study of the Sacraments, half the year on Baptism, half on Eucharist. In 2007, Carroll and the Session invited the congregation to a conversation about the Sacraments and how experience of them might be enriched. Forums for discussion included sermons, newsletter articles, and educational components. In Advent, the church celebrated the Lord's Supper every Sunday.

After Christmas, for several Sundays the bulletins included inserts asking people about their experience of weekly Communion during Advent. The response rate was only about 30 percent, but the responses were overwhelmingly positive, except for a few reservations related mostly to the length of the service. The Session wrestled with the question of length, but also identified for themselves other questions that might arise and used those as a structure for their own study.

During Eastertide when they were again celebrating the Supper weekly, the Session met three times, all the while in touch with the congregation both with surveys and by sharing readings developed by the pastor. During that period, the Session basically suspended any business that was not pressing and spent their entire time together talking about their eucharistic activity. By the time they approached the end of what had been intended to be only a seasonal series of celebrations, they saw no obstacle to making the practice permanent, resolving first to commune weekly for a full year. The pastor's commitment had been that the Session elders be wholly invested, knowing the Reformed theological tradition well enough to be able to describe First Church's sacramental orientation with authenticity, and their own personal investment in it.

By the end of the yearlong practice of weekly Eucharist, the intention was that the Session would have developed its own theological position about why they were doing what they were doing. Carroll insisted that it should not be eucharistic practice alone that would be scrutinized and evaluated, but everything being done in worship. Scrutiny was to be guided by these questions: Why do we do the things we do? Why do we make announcements orally that are already printed in the bulletin? Why do we ask for joys and concerns at the time that we do? At the end of the year of Communion every week, the congregation was invited to a dinner at church after worship to talk about their worship life, and the overwhelming response of the people was that they could no longer imagine not celebrating the Eucharist every Sunday.

One of five persons presented by the Presbytery as a potential designated pastor, Vice Moderator Tom Trinidad, now of Faith Church in Colorado Springs, was as direct with the committee that interviewed him as Andrus had been with his. He said to them, "You are starving your congregation by having quarterly Communion. If you call me to this church, I am from the first Sunday going to be talking about the importance of Communion, and keeping it up until we have weekly Communion." Some members of the interviewing committee were shocked, and others intrigued. Those who attended the early service, at which Eucharist was celebrated weekly, felt that their experience validated Trinidad's take on the situation.

When Trinidad began his pastorate at Faith, he tried to create a hunger for Communion at the 10:30 service by showing the link between the sermon the people had just heard and the meal, both of which had been experienced by the 8:15 congregation on that same morning. The intention was to plant a seed about how the enacted Sacrament complements and completes the Word proclaimed in Scripture and sermon.

A year later the congregation engaged a consulting group to help them evaluate where they were and where they might be. The consultants recommended that they combine the two services and, further, that the recommendation be put before the congregation within a set time. Trinidad facilitated eight open-invitation listening groups in homes or at the church, at which he laid out for the membership what the consultants had said and the reasoning behind their recommendation, without lobbying for it.

The usual reservations and obstacles surfaced, and there were clearly fears and uncertainties about the proposed change. However, as soon as Trinidad had arrived, the church had made the move from quarterly to monthly Communion without experiencing many complaints, so were not

Introducing Change Successfully

unused to change and not entirely averse to it. Upon the recommendation of the Session, the congregation resolved to accept the recommendation of the consultants. The members who worshiped regularly at the early service said, "Well, of course we're going to have weekly Communion." Those who worshiped at 10:30 had been hearing about this since Trinidad had begun his work there, and they consented.

Reservations were more often related to the change in worship times as they went from two services to one, and to concerns about the length of the new service as compared to what they had been used to in services that had been unequal in length. The 8:15 had been a fifty-minute service, and the 10:30 had been an hour. The new service would begin at 9:00 and end at 10:15. A few members left, not because of weekly Communion, but because they had liked the smallness of the 8:15 service and the earlier hour. Yet all in all, Faith Presbyterian is a congregation with a capacity for flexibility. Those who have left have been replaced in numbers—and more than replaced—by persons drawn to the congregation for many reasons, certainly including weekly Eucharist.

At West Plano Presbyterian Church, there had been weekly Eucharist at 8:30 from the beginning of that service in the early 1990s, but at 11:00 the practice was to celebrate the meal frequently but not every week. In fact, the meal was celebrated so frequently that there might be only three to five Sundays without Communion scattered here and there between sequences of weekly celebrations, and the irregularity simply became confusing. In May 2005 the Worship Committee recommended to the Session that the service of Word and Sacrament become established as normative for all Lord's Day services. The motion was defeated. The committee returned with a second motion, asking the Session to join them in working through the question of the normative form of worship for West Plano Church, keeping the issue on the table.

In October of 2006, a year in the lectionary cycle that included five sequential Sundays with Gospel texts from John 6 (eucharistic texts), Pastor Batchelder asked the Session to authorize the celebration of the Sacrament on September 10 in honor of the 9/11 tragedy, and suggested moving from there to weekly Communion. As it turned out, some of the *no* votes in 2005 had not expressed the conviction of the Session members themselves, but they had been making an effort to represent a few people in the congregation who had expressed such sentiments. In good faith, these Session members had believed it necessary to maintain some non-Eucharist Sundays as a gesture of pastoral concern for those who had indicated they would not welcome weekly Communion.

Once Batchelder learned that the elders' votes had not represented their personal conviction, he made it a point to visit with those in the congregation whom he knew to be reluctant. He was able to report to the Session that he had had conversation with those who preferred not to have weekly Communion, and that they had indicated that they would not be opposed. At that point, the Session decided by consensus (they are operating less by Robert's Rules of Order and more by consensus) to establish the service of Word and Sacrament as normative for all Lord's Day and festival-day services for a year. At the end of the year, the Session reflected on the experience and resolved to continue with weekly Eucharist. Issues about logistics had been worked out long ago, so none emerged in the course of these decisions. The work that had been required had to do with pastoral care and weighing the duties that come with leadership.

What If We Were to Try This?

Anyone who has ever been associated with more than one Presbyterian congregation has certainly discovered that there are big differences in congregational cultures, just as there are differences in the personalities, working styles, and experience of individual ministers. An experiment or two can reveal whether your congregation is more likely to be one to which change comes easily, or one more likely to proceed cautiously. The results might be a surprise to everyone. For example, one way of exposing congregations to alternative practices is by introducing them first at gatherings for worship outside the Sunday service. The women's retreat—or the men's or the youth's or the whole congregation's weekend at camp—may include the Lord's Supper, celebrated in ways that introduce new practices.

Often congregations are more open to something new during the summer, when attendance may be slimmer, people are in and out, and the usual protocols are more relaxed. Once some of the key participants in the congregation's life have crossed the boundary of customary practice, they may be better able to lead in welcoming (or consenting to) change when it is introduced on a more typical Sunday morning. Pastors can assess whether the congregation they serve is an early-adapter sort of congregation or one in which change takes a long time to ferment. Such assessment may involve the pastor or other leaders working with a long-range-planning committee, worship committee, or Session as a whole to set out a tentative timeline for reaching various stages in working toward a weekly celebration of the Lord's Supper, and that timeline may involve months or even years. Then steps may be taken to lead from one stage of the timeline to the next, with opportunities for learning, feedback, and reflection at every stage.

When asked how he accounted for the Edgewood congregation accepting changes in worship so easily, Pastor Sid Burgess offered his observation that in his childhood experience in a small Southern town, it had been taken for granted that everybody would go to church. "Now, everybody has to make a decision every Sunday whether or not to go to church because there are so many options. People really need to be able to cite a specific reason to come to our particular church on this particular Sunday. When change became the order of the Lord's Day at Edgewood, members had a reason to come each week to see what 'new thing' God was doing." For them, change seems to have been intriguing, appealing, and compelling.

NCDs are another story entirely, by contrast with long-established congregations. By the very nature of the case, their constituents expect something new. Those who are orienting or training potential organizing pastors for NCDs would do well to bear this in mind, incorporating into their curriculum careful attention to the *Directory for Worship*, with its endorsement of weekly Communion, as well as a review of Reformed and ecumenical sacramental theology, particularly in the light of very real generational change rooted in a major cultural paradigm shift. In this new era, which is in many ways more hospitable to the Sacraments than the modern era now being left behind, and less hospitable to the words-dominated models of our grandparents, now is not a time for timidity in reaching deep into our treasury of resources. Every problem, every obstacle, offers an opportunity for those with the courage to seek it.

Five

Where Are We Going and How Shall We Get There?

Weekly Communion at Other than Principal Services

Planning for Growth

In 1983, when I was pastor of Second Presbyterian Church in Lexington, Kentucky, a family in the church began to lobby for an early service as an alternative to the existing 11:00 a.m. service. It seemed a worthy effort, and offered an opportunity to introduce weekly Eucharist, an option supported both by the ministers and the organist. The interim pastor who had preceded me, upon finishing her work at Second Church in 1980, had advised the new pastor that this was a "sweet-tempered congregation," an observation that proved to be true for the most part, and neither the Worship Committee nor the Session offered any objection to the creation of an additional service. Since people would gather around the Table to commune, there would be no need to recruit elders to distribute the bread and cup in the pews, so the logistical details were worked out without much difficulty. People took turns in the relatively simple preparation and setting up.

A few years before, during an earlier pastorate, the congregation had given up its early service, identical to the second, due to dwindling attendance, and the associate pastor at that time was still a member of the staff when I was there in 1983. He cautioned that the decision to offer an early service was worth trying, but the decision should be reviewed within a specified time, and if there were not at least fifty people attending, it should be terminated. About eighteen people attended the first service, at 8:30 a.m., and although the numbers were seldom if ever fewer than that, the average attendance remained in the low twenties for several years. Nevertheless, the staff members were sufficiently committed to it that no consideration was given to calling off the service. By the time I left the congregation ten years later, in 1993, attendance was typically in the mideighties, and a decade after that, those present mostly filled the sanctuary with the exception of the balcony and transepts.

First learning: do not give up too soon. If conserving staff resources had been a primary objective, attendance would not have warranted the trouble, and the service would not have lasted six months. Second learning: hold the service in a space that makes room for growth. The 8:30 service at Second Church took place in the sanctuary, since there was no chapel or other appropriate space for it. If there had been a smaller space available, no doubt the service would have been housed there, and the likelihood is that it would not have grown much beyond the small group with which it began.

A number of careful observers have noted that a worship space will rarely fill to beyond 80 percent of capacity, with the exception of rare occasions like Christmas and Easter, and some configurations will not be filled beyond 65 percent. For example, if pews run directly up to an outer wall people feel trapped, and if the ceiling is low, the space will look smaller than it is. At 65-percent full, and even at 80 percent, the space may appear to have room for additional worshipers, but the psychology is such that people will not be comfortable in what are perceived to be close quarters, and attendance will cut off at that point. Many services offered early on Sunday or at an afternoon or evening hour on Saturday or Sunday will never grow beyond a certain point when they have been located in a chapel or other space that will not permit growth beyond a maximum of 80 percent of capacity. Once capacity reaches that point, it needs to be moved to a larger space, or it will seem both to newcomers and ongoing members that the service has been created with the expectation that it should remain small.

Corey Nelson, one of the associate pastors at First Presbyterian Church, Lake Forest, Illinois, introduced a service of weekly Eucharist at 5:00 p.m. on Sunday afternoons, and although attendance is much smaller than the two morning services, the afternoon service is held in the sanctuary. Lighting is adjusted in such a way as to accent the space at the front of the sanctuary where the worshipers are expected to sit, and where the center of action is. Lighting in the back of the sanctuary is extinguished, but with full lighting in the front, the space both beckons and seems smaller. Light, in fact, plays a significant role in this service, including the lighting of candles early in the service, while the people are singing the opening hymn or chorus. Following the call to worship, Corey Nelson offers a word about the various symbolic meanings of light, and those present are invited to come forward to light candles in candleholders that hang on a kind of screen, each screen with thirty-six votive cups. Most worshipers come forward, strike a match and light a candle, extinguishing the match in a bowl of water.

Nelson had lived for a time in Louisville and attended the Covenant Community NCD, where Jud Hendrix had been organizing pastor, and Corey consulted with Jud and others there as he took the initiative to shape this new 5:00 p.m. service in Lake Forest, a Chicago suburb, following their model. At First Church, the two morning services are scheduled at 9:00 a.m. and 11:00 a.m., with a concurrent education hour during the first service. The Lord's Supper is celebrated on the first Sunday of the month. Attendance at the two morning services equals a little less than a third of the total number of members recorded, very typical for larger churches, and efforts to increase that number had little effect. Nelson, whose job description is Associate Pastor for Mission, wondered whether another service with a different style or at a different time might be worth a try to see if it would be possible to reach out to more of their existing members.

Across the street from the church is Lake Forest College, founded by the same people who founded the church, and identified by the PCUSA as a denominationally related institution. First Church has been trying to grow a ministry to the campus, with the intention of being a welcoming place for college students coming from a variety of religious traditions and looking for a faith community. Some of those involved in launching the 5:00 p.m. service saw college students as a targeted constituency, and some students have indeed responded. Students make up somewhere between 15 percent and 25 percent of those worshiping at that hour. But Nelson's primary concern has been to connect with people on the rolls who do not worship on Sunday mornings.

Of course, the Covenant Community congregation, where Corey Nelson had worshiped during his time in Louisville, celebrates the Eucharist weekly, but for Nelson, the practice is more than just following the precedent he experienced there. "More than the practicalities," he observes, weekly Eucharist is "the theological piece for me." He has been reading Sara Miles, once an atheist, now an articulate and missionally minded Christian based at St. Gregory of Nyssa, an experimental and in many ways atypical Episcopal parish in San Francisco.[1] Out of her church Miles began a feeding program that has grown exponentially, and Nelson is impressed with her language about the meaning and power of the Eucharist. As a former educator, Nelson loves taking part in the rite every week, and believes that there is a multisensory, tactile element to it that appeals to people in a way that the spoken or sung word does not do.

Some families with children or teenagers prefer the 5:00 p.m. service because they appreciate worshiping together. At 9:00 in the morning the younger generation is likely to be in church school, and if they should attend with their parents at 11:00, they do not always feel able to relate. (The process of effectively excommunicating baptized children until adolescence, substituting either church school or a so-called children's service for the gathered community at worship, is self-defeating. Designating separate precincts and programs for children while the congregation gathers makes the worship of the congregation alien to those who have been largely excluded until their teen years.) The energy and format at the 5:00 p.m. service are engaging for many children and youth. The evening service features the use of a projection screen, and a small musical ensemble leads music from a variety of traditions. Projected onto the screen are images and video, the words for musical pieces, and liturgical materials. No printed bulletin is employed, although the same bulletin insert available in the morning services is distributed in order to share announcements and news of the congregation. Nelson, a former high school band and choir director, leads the singing, with a couple other singers, a guitar, piano, and African drum.

Members of the congregation come forward to commune by intinction, using a fresh loaf of rustic French or Italian bread from a bakery. The presiding minister, usually Nelson, breaks the bread and places a good-sized piece of it in each person's hands. Another server holds the cup, which is filled with grape juice. Except for an occasional Taizé chant, the people do not ordinarily sing as they come forward, but the ensemble plays, usually from the standard contemporary Christian repertoire.

Those who attend this service include children and teenagers with their parents, who are for the most part among the early members of Generation X, the generation that follows the Baby Boomers. A few empty

---

1. Miles, *Take This Bread*.

nesters who were involved in the church when their children were young, but stopped coming to worship after their children grew up, returned to worship when this service began. Some families come with small children who remain throughout. A few couples of retirement age attend this service as well.

Once again following the pattern of Covenant Community in Louisville, a meal follows every evening service at First Church in Lake Forest, with no advance reservations required. The meal is usually homemade, prepared by a team of volunteers, and there is no charge. (The church has a budget item to reimburse expenses for the volunteers who cook, although some donate the cost of the meal.) About half of those present for worship remain for the meal, including almost all the college students, who have bonded and look forward to that time.

Maximizing Opportunities

When Steve Montgomery became pastor of Idlewild Presbyterian Church in Memphis in 2000, the congregation was accustomed to quarterly Communion at both the 8:30 and 11:00 a.m. services as well as Communion on Maundy Thursday and Christmas Eve. Montgomery led discussions with the Worship Committee looking more closely at sacramental theology in the Reformed tradition, hoping to find a way to introduce more frequent celebration. The result was a compromise, moving from quarterly to monthly Communion at 11:00 a.m. and weekly celebrations at 8:30 a.m. By the time a motion came to the Session, they engaged in a little more theological discussion but for the most part had reached the point where the questions were mainly about nuts and bolts: "So, who's going to do all this anyway?"

Attendance at the 8:30 service had begun to dwindle, but when weekly Eucharist was instituted, that service began to attract people who wanted more frequent Communion, some of them former Episcopalians, Catholics, or Lutherans. The congregation began going forward to commune, by intinction, and, though it was a change from previous practice, the people liked it. Montgomery comments that "you feel more a part of the community when you see the other people you're worshiping with, and it's helped our 8:30 service grow . . . It seemed to be almost a 'perfect storm' of really good things coming together at the right time." Attendance has about doubled.

Attenders at 8:30 used to be mostly older people, but now a few families with children are present, as well as a number of young adults without children. "Demographics, age-wise, have changed pretty dramatically," Montgomery notes. "Now it's pretty evenly distributed between a number of twenties and thirties, and some middle-aged folks and some older, retired types."

The Idlewild Church has a third service, also with weekly Communion, on Thursday evenings. It follows a meal scheduled for 5:30 p.m. at which they feed about a hundred homeless persons or other people frequently defined as working poor, who are invited but certainly not required to come to the service following, which lasts about thirty minutes. Most accept the invitation. At Communion, the worshipers gather in a circle and pass the bread and then the cup. One of the leaders of this service is Kendra Hotz, a faculty member at Presbyterian-related Rhodes College, and an ordained PCUSA minister. She recruits from among the guests those willing to take roles in the service, and in her sermons often draws a connection between the meal that preceded the service and the Eucharist. On the fourth Thursday of the month, Gayle Walker, an associate pastor, leads the service, and on that evening it includes a Service for Wholeness. All those present are invited to come forward, if they wish, perhaps to kneel, for prayer and anointing with oil.

The Memphis congregation has recently started a monthly service called the Festival, held at 5:00 p.m. on a Sunday evening in the Fellowship hall. According to the church website, a worship service that includes the Lord's Supper is followed by a potluck supper.[2] The intention is to be specific in drawing a link between both kinds of table fellowship. Pastor Montgomery notes that the congregation in that service has included visitors such as a couple of Roman Catholic women who work as nurses and cannot attend their own church because they work weekend shifts.

At the 11:00 service at Idlewild, half the time the bread and cup are served in the pews, and half the time the people come forward and commune by intinction. The 11:00 congregation hears the same sermon as the 8:30 congregation in which there is weekly Eucharist, so the sermons at both services are likely to include some reference to the meal. Weekly Communion at 8:30 has heightened Steve Montgomery's sensitivity to preaching embedded in a eucharistic context; i.e., he is attentive to the ecology

---

2. Information is available on the website for Idlewild Presbyterian Church in Memphis: http://www.idlewildchurch.org/worshipschedules#festival/.

of Word and Sacrament, each reacting to the other. The relation between Table fellowship and hospitality affects his preaching.

The Presbyterian Church of Sewickley, Pennsylvania, near Pittsburgh, is one of many congregations with an early service celebrating Eucharist every Sunday. It began in the summer of 1992 in response to the desire for more frequent Communion on the part of members of the congregation and the church staff. Until 2000, weekly Communion was a practice limited to the early service in summertime, but in the fall of that year became a feature of the 8:00 a.m. service all year long.

Weekly Eucharist at this service has become established practice and is valued by the Session, the Worship and Music Committee, the staff, and a number of members of the congregation. Worshipers come forward to commune by intinction.

Fourth Presbyterian Church in Chicago, a church of more than five thousand members, offers two services with weekly Eucharist in addition to its two principal services on Sunday morning. Adam H. Fronczek, Associate Pastor for Adult Education and Worship, reports that after 9/11, when attendance spiked, an 8:00 a.m. service was added. At first John Buchanan, the pastor at the time, who has since retired, preached at that service as well as at the other two morning services. As Buchanan began to reduce his role in preparation for retirement, the preaching responsibility at 8:00 a.m. was delegated to other ministers on the staff. To distinguish this service, they developed a different choir for it and added weekly Communion. Some, not favoring that move, chose another service, but an equal number began attending because they were attracted to it. Those attending the service now represent a good mix of ages and circumstances, including some single young adults as well as a large number of older adults, who have always been well represented.

The 8:00 a.m. service is held in the church sanctuary. Ushers rope off the back two-thirds of the large space, and most people sit in the first twenty rows. The congregation rises and comes forward for Communion, by intinction, using ordinary sliced bread and grape juice.

The other service at Fourth Church that includes weekly Eucharist is held in the sanctuary at 4:00 p.m., and is a jazz service, featuring improvisational jazz played by a quartet. This service includes all the standard elements of a Reformed service, but the musical style and casual nature distinguish it from other services at Fourth. The congregation sings responses, and sometimes an antiphonal psalm, as well as the sung pieces of the eucharistic liturgy (the Sanctus, etc.), all led by the jazz ensemble.

Where Are We Going and How Shall We Get There?

The 4:00 p.m. service resulted when it became necessary to rethink and redesign a service customarily scheduled for 6:30 p.m. on Sundays, one that was basically the same as the morning services except that it included weekly Communion. The intention when moving to 4:00 p.m. was to reach out to people who were essentially unchurched. In fact, the people who attend that service do not represent that demographic exclusively since it has proven to attract a more diverse congregation than expected. A high percentage of young adults both single and partnered have been drawn to that service. There are young people and old, people who come singly and some with families, straight and gay couples. The congregation is ethnically diverse and includes a good representation of Asians and African Americans. Attendance at this service has grown steadily. Although all the services at Fourth typically draw a large number of visitors, at least half of those coming at 4:00 p.m. are members or at least regular constituents of Fourth Church, and their numbers are steadily rising.

The communicants go forward to commune, as they do at the 8:00 a.m. service. It has been made clear to the jazz musicians that the intention is for the Lord's Supper to be a celebration, and the music played during communion supports that.

The Gayton Kirk in Henrico, Virginia, where Janet James is pastor, is a small PCUSA congregation that nevertheless offers three Sunday services, two of which include weekly Eucharist. The 8:30 a.m. service is styled as a Celtic service, making use of special arrangements of Celtic music, with a guided discussion of the Scripture of the day, concluding with Communion. The 5:00 p.m. service is called jazz vespers, and also includes weekly Communion. A jazz trio leads the music. The Scripture readings are interpreted with the use of art and poetry. Worshipers sit at small tables during this service, which leads directly to a simple meal of soup and bread, accompanied by discussion.

Implications of Adding a Eucharistic Service

Many examples can be found of services with weekly Eucharist at an hour earlier than the usual late Sunday morning service in Presbyterian congregations, whether in Lincoln, Nebraska, or Los Angeles or Atlanta or Wilson, North Carolina, or Bryn Mawr, Pennsylvania—in churches both large and small. A few offer such a service on Sunday afternoon or evening, or on Saturday evening or during the week. Having initiated early services with weekly Eucharist in two Presbyterian congregations, I wonder whether adding such a service to the worship menu of a congregation serves the greater cause of eventually achieving weekly Communion in the principal service or subverts it? Does the very presence of one service that consistently celebrates both Word and Sacrament every week lead to complacency—as though, with this goal achieved, it is no longer urgent to press on for the greater one? Or, on the other hand, does the very fact that such a service exists in a congregation serve to familiarize the whole congregation with the fact that weekly Communion is a live possibility even for Presbyterians? Does a weekly Communion service possibly function as a standing rebuttal of the traditional objections so that weekly Communion no longer seems strange? Does such a service thus help to break down potential resistance to moving toward Word and Sacrament in every Lord's Day service?

Several of the congregations in this study began with two services: an early service—usually smaller—with weekly Communion, and a later one normally without it. But for various reasons these congregations eventually chose to combine the two services and practice weekly Communion. The experience of weekly Communion does more to persuade the uncertain than the most clever arguments for it, and so those who have become accustomed to it become strong advocates when two different services become one. The presence of a service of weekly Eucharist in a congregation does seem to raise the sacramental consciousness of a congregation, including the consciousness of those who never attend it, and it certainly stimulates the thinking of Sessions and worship committees. Ideally, adding such a service would be a first step, with the larger goal of increasing frequency at the principal service until the goal of weekly Communion has been reached. Pursuit of this goal will require long-range thinking that includes assessment of the role that an existing service of weekly Word and Sacrament may play as planners work steadily toward the larger goal—weekly Eucharist at the principal service, if not at all services.

It is rather remarkable how the firmly fixed tradition of quarterly Communion has given way to monthly Communion over the past three to five decades. According to General Assembly statistics for 2012, in that year 69.3 percent of PCUSA congregations celebrated the meal at least on a monthly basis, as compared, for example, to 53 percent in 1997. Congregations have experienced what is really a monumental shift from four Communions a year (on Sunday morning) to twelve times a year, three times as often as before, and very often that shift has occurred all at once. What

Where Are We Going and How Shall We Get There?

it has done is to make the old objections about losing something special harder to sustain, since tripling the number of Communion occasions has made the Sacrament less rare but not less valued. The fact that most congregations moved from quarterly in one year to monthly in the next indicates that it is not as difficult as we might have imagined for congregations to consent to a rather dramatic change, and then, over time, to regard the new practice as the way it is meant to be.

What Can We Learn from Episcopal and Lutheran Experience?

The Episcopal Church

If you were to visit an Episcopal Church on a Sunday morning in, say, 1950, it is almost certain that the principal service would be Morning Prayer. Morning Prayer did not originate as a service specifically for Sunday, the Lord's Day, but grows out of the Daily Offices prayed in monastic communities several times every day. In Episcopal usage, it was typical to add a Sunday sermon, which, in monastic services of daily prayer would have been optional and often omitted. If you were to have checked the parish's weekly calendar, it would not be at all surprising were you to discover that early on Sunday morning—sometimes very early—there would also be a service of Holy Communion, often without music.

However, if you were to visit an Episcopal Church next Sunday morning, well into the twenty-first century, you would be almost certain to find that there will be two services, both called The Holy Eucharist, one using Rite One, the other Rite Two, the difference being that Rite One continues to use the language of the King James Bible, whereas Rite Two uses contemporary language. Rite Two is typically the larger, more popular service.

By the year 2001, the percentage of Episcopal congregations offering only Morning Prayer on Sundays was only 0.9 percent, and most of those churches (57 reporting) celebrate a Eucharist during the week. That number has varied only slightly since 1991, the year of the oldest electronic records.[3] C. Kirk Hadaway, Congregational Research Officer for The Episcopal Church, recalls reading about times long past when bishops might

---

3. E-mail from C. Kirk Hadaway, PhD, Officer, Congregational Research, The Episcopal Church, January 24, 2013.

be called papists for encouraging Holy Communion every week. What happened?

It is hard to put a finger on the precise causes behind this rather dramatic change, but the adoption of a revised *Book of Common Prayer* in 1979 might serve as well as any to mark a kind of watershed moment that both stimulated change and at the same time represented changes that had already been in process throughout much of the twentieth century. James Farwell, Associate Professor of Theology and Liturgy at Virginia Theological Seminary, notes that "on the eve of the new prayer book's adoption, it was not uncommon to find the Eucharist being celebrated once a month, or on the first and third Sunday of the month. In more 'low church' dioceses like Virginia, for example, Eucharist was much more infrequent."[4]

Officially, at least, responsibility and authority for liturgy and music in a parish resides with the Rector, according to Farwell. Although adding or eliminating weekly Eucharist requires no vote from the Vestry or a worship committee, it is clearly true for Episcopalians as for everyone else that the mere fact of possessing authority means little unless stakeholders support a Rector's decisions.

Of course, the Episcopal Church, like most of the major confessional bodies, has been influenced by twentieth-century scholarship that included the biblical theology movement and the ecumenical movement that brought in its train increased interest in the study of the history and theology of Christian worship, including a recovery of sacramental theology. For some twenty years prior to the adoption of the new prayer book, the Episcopal Church had circulated a series of Prayer Book Studies that reflected the new scholarship, published under the authority of its General Convention. The Prayer Book Studies reflected the informed thinking of a Standing Commission of the General Convention whose responsibility was to deal with liturgy. In the early 1970s, two major trial prayer books became available for experimental use in the church, leading to the adoption of a new *Book of Common Prayer* in 1979.

The 1979 *Book of Common Prayer* describes The Holy Eucharist as "the principal act of Christian worship on the Lord's Day and other major Feasts," in contrast to the 1928 prayer book, which reads that "the Order for Holy Communion, the Order for Morning Prayer, the Order for Evening Prayer, and the Litany . . . are the regular Services appointed for Public Worship in this Church."[5] The change in language marks a significant shift,

---

4. E-mail to the author, January 1, 2013.

5. Episcopal Church, *BCP* (1979) 13; Episcopal Church, *BCP* (1928), vii.

Where Are We Going and How Shall We Get There?

indicating that the Eucharist is to be considered normative for the principal Sunday worship of the church. Weekly Eucharist is not required by church law, and churches exist for which Morning Prayer remains the principal service, but the fact that the vast majority of Episcopal parishes have followed the lead represented in the revised 1979 prayer book indicates that a new consensus has emerged. It is not surprising that such a thing might happen in that church, since the *Book of Common Prayer* has served as a major identifier of what it is to be Episcopalian, and Episcopalians tend to grant a good measure of authority to those who have both shaped and interpreted their worship.

Lutheran Experience

The Evangelical Lutheran Church in America (ELCA), another Reformation church, like our own, is one of the churches in full communion with the PCUSA, meaning that we can easily participate fully in one another's worship and share ministers as well. A Lutheran pastor who graduated from seminary in 1973 describes Communion once a month as, at that time, "an unquestioned norm."[6]

In 1978, two of the three Lutheran bodies that would eventually come together to form the ELCA, the American Lutheran Church and the Lutheran Church in America, both approved "A Statement of Communion Practices." Under "Frequency of Celebration," this document cites a Lutheran confessional document that testifies to the historic Reformation practice of weekly Communion, and encourages congregations to move toward that goal. The same year, the Inter-Lutheran Commission on Worship published *Lutheran Book of Worship*.[7] The *LBW* differed from its predecessors in that the texts for the service, titled "The Holy Communion," are printed in such a way as to suggest that Communion is the norm, whereas not celebrating it was the unusual/infrequent option.[8] In 1988, three Lutheran bodies—the American Lutheran Church, the Lutheran Church in America, and the Association of Evangelical Lutheran Churches—came together to form the ELCA.

The newly formed church adopted "A Statement of Communion Practices" in 1988, the year in which the union was consummated. In 1995,

6. E-mail from Ronald Luckey, December 10, 2012.
7. Lutheran Church in America, *LBW*.
8. E-mail from Gordon Lathrop, December 20, 2012.

seven years after the formation of the ELCA, the new church adopted another document called "The Use of the Means of Grace," which includes Principle 35: "According to the Apology of the Augsburg Confession, Lutheran congregations celebrate the Holy Communion every Sunday and festival. This confession remains the norm for our practice," and the statement that "all of our congregations are encouraged to celebrate the Lord's Supper weekly, but not every service need be a Eucharist."[9]

Like the PCUSA, the ELCA collects information from local congregations, and, beginning in 1989, a year after the formation of the new church, the chuch began asking a question about the frequency of Communion. That year, approximately 17 percent of ELCA churches celebrated the meal weekly, the next largest group (about 29 percent) celebrating once a month plus festivals. About 15 percent celebrated the Supper once a month, and a very small number celebrated quarterly.[10] The denomination asked the question about frequency of Communion again four years later, in 1993, and by then the number of churches celebrating weekly had risen to about 18.5 percent. After that, the question was asked every two years, with continuing increases in the percentage of churches celebrating the meal weekly every time. The largest jump occurred in 2000, when the number grew to 29 percent, perhaps showing increasing familiarity with *The Use of the Means of Grace*.[11] Significant increases continued every two years until in 2008, the last time the denomination queried congregations about frequency, when the percentage of weekly-Eucharist congregations reached to slightly over 50 percent. If increases have been continuing at the same rate, the number should have reached nearly 70 percent by 2013.

The ELCA produced a new hymnal and service book, *Evangelical Lutheran Worship*, in 2006. In this book, the primary service, Holy Communion, is printed in such a way as to presume that the whole service of Word and Sacrament will be celebrated, with no suggestion that the service might be truncated to a Service of the Word alone. *ELW* instead adds, following ten settings for Holy Communion, an order for a Service of the Word, with the notation, "This Service of the Word derives its pattern from the service of Holy Communion. Although a weekly celebration of the Lord's Supper

---

9. Evangelical Lutheran Church in America, *Principles*, 125.

10. Evangelical Lutheran Church in America, Research Office, "Frequency of Communion for ELCA Congregations" (statistical chart obtained directly from the Research and Evaluation Office of the ELCA).

11. Ibid.

is the norm, a service of the word of God is also celebrated regularly or occasionally in many places."[12] For Presbyterians, who pride ourselves on the freedom to adapt worship to local circumstances, it may come as a surprise to read in the Introduction to *ELW*, quoting from *LBW*, "*Evangelical Lutheran Worship* continues to emphasize that 'freedom and flexibility in worship is a Lutheran inheritance, and there is room for ample variety in ceremony, music, and liturgical form.'"[13]

In a local congregation of the ELCA, authority in matters such as how frequently to celebrate the Eucharist rests, typically, with the Congregation Council. However, the ELCA is more loosely governed in local decision-making than the PCUSA. As in other denominations, so in the ELCA the pastor is likely to have a great deal of influence over decisions related to worship, but not to the extent of being indifferent to the feelings of the congregation.

The PCUSA

Just as the Lutheran story unfolds differently from the Episcopal story, so will the Presbyterian story proceed according to its own history and polity. Episcopalians and Lutherans both have identified themselves, at least in part, by their adherence to forms of worship that stem from single sources from the Reformation era: Cranmer's 1549 *Book of Common Prayer* in the case of Episcopalians; and, although less authoritative, Luther's *Formula Missae* (1523) for Lutherans. While the Reformed also created service books quite as early as Lutherans and Anglicans, and used them in much the same way, our worship does not originate in a single source, since the several Swiss and Scottish reformers created their own liturgies. In the Reformed case, the primary objective was simplicity and comprehensibility rather than either verbal or ceremonial continuity, or even a concern for aesthetics. That is quite understandable, given the context and the predilections of the reformers involved, and yet, not likely to leave a legacy as enduring as either Cranmer's or Luther's. Add to that the fact that Scottish Presbyterianism abandoned Knox's liturgy (modeled after Calvin's Geneva liturgy) when the Scots became infected with a rather viral form of Puritanism, strengthened by both Scottish resentment of the English, and Puritan objections to the Church of England and anything resembling its worship.

12. Evangelical Lutheran Church in America, *ELW*, 210.
13. Ibid., 8.

The result was that Presbyterians, ever since the Westminster Assembly in 1644, inherited some rather vague rubrics rather than a specific form of worship and, even though American Presbyterians have had a *Book of Common Worship* since 1906, our practice has proven not easily changed by either a more specific *Directory for Worship* or a magnificent liturgical resource like the 1993 *BCW*.

Even when the 1961 revision of the *Directory for Worship* added, for the first time, the statement that "it is fitting that [the Lord's Supper] be observed as frequently as on each Lord's Day . . ." (and in today's *Directory*, "It is appropriate to celebrate the Lord's Supper as often as each Lord's Day"),[14] the language suggests that weekly Communion is permissible, even admirable, but does not make a stronger statement that a service of both Word and Sacrament ought to be normative. The *BCW* states that "the Eucharist is increasingly recognized as central to the liturgy on the Lord's Day, and there is steady movement toward weekly celebration."[15] However, like the Lutheran *Service Book and Hymnal*, a 1958 predecessor to *LBW*, the *BCW* is printed in such a way as to suggest that the Lord's Supper is an optional part of the Service for the Lord's Day. A rubric on page 66 reads, "If the Lord's Supper is not to be celebrated, the Service continues on Page 79."[16] The Service for the Lord's Day is printed in the new Presbyterian hymnal, *Glory to God*, preceded by the stronger statement that "the Service for the Lord's Day is a service of Word and Sacrament. Together they form a unified liturgy; one is incomplete without the other."[17] In the Eucharist section of the service, following the Offering and preceding the Invitation to the Table, is a notation that "The norm of Christian worship is to celebrate the Lord's Supper on each Lord's Day. If the Lord's Supper is omitted. . . ."[18] In other words, the Service for the Lord's Day is more definitively framed as a single service of Word and Sacrament as normative, though not quite as uncompromisingly as in *ELW*.

Presbyterians and other Reformed have been part of the liturgical reform movement that has developed ecumenically over more than one hundred years, and have shared in the benefits of its biblical and historical scholarship and contributed to such scholarship quite as much as have all

---

14. W-2.4009.
15. Presbyterian Church (USA), *BCW*, 7.
16. Ibid., 66.
17. Presbyterian Church (USA), *Glory to God*, 1.
18. Ibid., 8.

Where Are We Going and How Shall We Get There?

the major historic confessions, both Catholic and Protestant. For historical rather than theological reasons, the move toward weekly Eucharist is more of an uphill battle for Presbyterians than it has been for either Episcopalians or Lutherans, but there is certainly movement, nevertheless. For example, in 1950 quarterly Communion was the norm, whereas in 2013, nearly 70 percent of PCUSA congregations celebrate the Supper at least monthly. This is a dramatic change.

Another sign that Presbyterians are on a journey similar to that of Episcopalians and Lutherans is that the shape of our Lord's Day worship more often than not follows the form of the Service for the Lord's Day even when there is no Communion. Before the Service for the Lord's Day, a Presbyterian service was likely to look very different on a Communion Sunday than it did on other Sundays. Most Sundays, the service reached its climax in the sermon, followed by a hymn and a Benediction. On Communion Sundays, the service was entirely different, often drawn from the 1946 *Book of Common Worship*. In the 1946 *BCW*, the Table of Contents lists six orders for Morning Worship, five for Evening Worship, plus two Services for Children and two for Young People, five Litanies and the Ten Commandments before it lists The Sacraments and Ordinances of the Church, in which section "The Lord's Supper or Holy Communion" is only the sixth item. The norm was clearly a service of the Word. Today, when the Service for the Lord's Day is the only Lord's Day service in the 1993 *BCW*, most churches reproduce its shape and form more or less consistently on every Sunday even when there is no Communion. In that case, following the pattern of the Service for the Lord's Day, the sermon is followed by the Creed, Prayers of the People, and Offering (the first movement of the specifically eucharistic action). Accordingly, it is possible to perceive the service, as both Calvin and the drafters of the Service for the Lord's Day intended, as missing something on non-Communion Sundays rather than as being an entirely different species of worship. The consistent use of a service shaped along classical ecumenical and Reformed lines as one of both Word and Sacrament lays the groundwork for the next step.

Reports from the Presbyterian Panel, created by the Presbyterian Mission Agency's Office of Research, tell us that in 1997, 2 percent of respondents belonged to congregations in the PCUSA that celebrated the Lord's Supper in at least one service every week.[19] By 2004, only seven years later, 5

---

19. Presbyterian Church (USA), *Session Annual Statistical Report Supplement End of Year 1997*.

percent of respondents reported belonging to congregations that celebrated the meal in at least one service every week, more than doubling the number reported in 1997.[20] In a 2009 survey, 9 percent of pastors reported celebrating weekly Communion.[21] However, the Presbyterian Panel surveys seek responses from a representative sample of individual pastors, elders, members, and specialized ministers rather than from specific congregations. In 2012, the annual questionnaire the Office of Research Services sent to Session clerks along with the General Assembly's Statistical Annual Form asked the clerks for the first time to answer questions related to frequency of the Lord's Supper, and 25 percent of responding congregations[22] indicated that they celebrated the meal weekly in at least one service every Sunday, the vast majority in other than the principal (most attended) service. Many other congregations indicated that, in addition to their stated Communion Sundays, they also celebrate the Supper on festival days and, in some cases, every Sunday during one or more liturgical seasons.[23] What we see is a slow but steady increase, and it appears that the increase is gaining strength more than incrementally.

Is our church moving toward a tipping point? A staff writer for the *New Yorker* magazine wrote a book several years ago called *The Tipping Point: How Little Things Can Make a Big Difference*.[24] He pointed out that while a community or institution can stay relatively stable for a long time, small changes can lead to a tipping point at which the pace of change picks up dramatically. Why, for example, does the crime rate in a depressed community suddenly decline? It may be as simple as a new community basketball program, or the introduction of community policing, where police officers on foot are trained to interact positively with the community, leading, over time, to a tipping point. No change is visible over a period of days, weeks, or months, and then at some moment impossible to pinpoint, when a tipping point is reached, crime decreases dramatically. Or, in a neglected neighborhood, where expectations are low and hope is hard to find, someone organizes a group of people to repair broken windows and paint over graffiti. Even though the change may be imperceptible from day to

---

20. Presbyterian Church (USA), *Session Annual Statistical Report Supplement End of Year 2004*.

21. Presbyterian Church (USA), *The Sacraments*.

22. The response rate was 67 percent.

23. Presbyterian Church (USA), *Clerk's Annual Questionnaire*.

24. Gladwell, *Tipping Point*.

day, a moment comes when the people of the neighborhood, seeing their surroundings cared for, begin to perceive their neighborhood differently, marking a tipping point when they exhibit a readiness to take it back from the forces of decay and hopelessness.

Similarly, most pastors discover that in the first months or even years of a new pastorate, things move very slowly, and it seems as though what needs to be done will never be done. And then, the pastoral relationship jells and a tipping point is reached after which what had seemed impossible becomes possible, and often even remarkably easy.

One may hope that the PCUSA is inching its way toward a tipping-point at which it will become more common than not that our congregations will celebrate—not observe, not serve, but celebrate—the Lord's Supper alongside the proclamation of the Word every week. When that happens, it will have more positive impact on our denominational future than anything else, whether resolution of a controversy or implementation of a strategic plan, or amendment of the *Book of Order*. It is not a silver bullet that will make our numbers soar as they did in the 1950s, but it will deepen our discipleship and signal that we are ready to embrace the postmodern world, with its readiness for an embodied, incarnational, and therefore more intensely biblical spirituality.

Six

Owning the Practice

When a congregation owns the practice of weekly Communion, it begins to make an impact on other aspects of congregational life. When youth from Edgewood Church in Birmingham, Alabama, go to Presbyterian conferences at Montreat, they are astonished to discover that not every Presbyterian church celebrates the meal every week. When young people from West Plano Church in Texas go off to college and seek out a Presbyterian congregation, they are shocked to find that there will, most Sundays, be no Sacrament. What seems exotic to most Presbyterians seems wholly natural to those who have grown up with it, so it is worthwhile to take note of how children experience weekly Word and Sacrament.

In new-member classes, confirmation classes, and other educational settings, most Presbyterian congregations deal either often or occasionally with interpreting sacramental theology and practice, but the context for sacramental education will be different in weekly-Eucharist congregations.

Most of our church sanctuaries were designed and constructed to serve the purposes of a congregation who would, for the most part, come in and sit down and remain more or less in place for the duration of a service. Neither architects nor building committees imagined a space in which room would be provided for large groups of people to move around. For the most part, with a little imagination it is not too difficult to find ways to use existing spaces differently than originally expected. Most churches that have moved to weekly or near-weekly Eucharist find it easier and more appealing for the people to rise from their places and process to stations where servers will offer the bread and cup (or individual cups), even if the building committee never imagined such a use. Some have even made changes in the worship space to heighten awareness of the Sacraments or to facilitate the movement of the congregation.

Presbyterians tend to seek out appropriate means to reach out in service to people in need in their communities, and often do that in ways that involve either the distribution of food or the provision of meals. Do churches that keep the holy meal every week sense any link between the Table and all the other tables?

Children at the Table

At the Madison Avenue Church a woman born in Poland, whose husband is a member of the congregation, cannot go back to the Roman Catholic Church because she has married a divorced man. When she came forward in the communion line, bringing with her a babe in arms, she asked pastor Fred Anderson for a blessing in lieu of the bread and cup. Anderson offered her a blessing, and she then asked him to bless her child. Many in New York City are reluctant to leave small children in the church nursery, since often parents are required to spend so much of every day apart from them, and now many parents bring very young children for a blessing. When someone came forward with a baby who had been baptized, Anderson later explained to the parents that he would, of course, be happy to offer a blessing to the child, but she could begin communing right now as long as the parents would be responsible to raise her to grow into an awareness of the Supper as a Sacrament and not just a snack. It is now common at Madison Avenue for three-year-olds to come forward, extending their hands for the bread, and they are completely at home communing along with all the other baptized. By the time these children get to a confirmation class, they have been eating and drinking at the Table all their lives.

At West Plano, children commune from the time of their Baptism, and the church begins to prepare parents for this as part of prebaptismal instruction. Children learn to come forward for the bread and cup, making a little throne with their hands. David Batchelder notes that at West Plano the practice is to group Baptisms at Easter, and sometimes on the Sunday known as Baptism of the Lord. Most young families prefer Baptism at the Saturday night Easter Vigil. In early centuries, the Sacrament of Baptism always led the newly baptized directly to the Eucharist, and at West Plano the close relationship between the two Sacraments is marked.

At Edgewood Church in Birmingham, "we welcome children long before they have any idea what it's all about," explains Sid Burgess. And yet, of course there is more than one way of "knowing what it's all about." Just as a very small child intuits what it is to belong to her family (or to be excluded from it) at mealtime, she also senses what it is to belong at the church's Table. It is possible to experience a Sacrament profoundly even if one is unable—or not yet able, or no longer able—to translate the experience into words. God is in search of us before we have given even a thought to holy things, reaching out to us before we are able to speak God's name. This truth is represented at the Table as much as at the font.

Brant Copeland, of First Church in Tallahassee, believes that participation in the communal meal is "absolutely vital to forming young Christians as disciples. It enables them to participate formally exactly the way all the other members are doing. It says to them, You belong, you're a part of this community." Copeland has observed that in the few times that the bread and cup are served in the pews, it confuses children. "Why aren't we getting to our feet?" When there is no Communion, they ask the obvious question, "How come there's no meal today?" And, Copeland says, "There's no good answer."

At Peace Church, Pastor Elizabeth Deibert hears occasionally from members shaped in the old school who believe that children should have participated in formal instruction before being permitted to participate. The church offers such instruction, but "I tell them all the time that it's the participation that teaches us. It's sitting around the dinner table at home that teaches you what a family is, and what it means to love one another as you sit together at a table, and the same with the church," Deibert explains. She cites Christian educator John Westerhoff, noting that his "'belonging' stage of faith is already happening when there's a regular experience of the Sacrament that children are participating in." There is often a child or two who is reluctant to dip the bread into the cup, and, says Deibert, "we try to encourage the parents to relax about that. Don't make a big deal about it, just let them enjoy the bread. I see a lot of joy on children's faces as they come."

At New Covenant Fellowship in Austin, where James Lee is pastor, children are dismissed from the service for education, but they return for Communion, and they are served first. "They get excited as they stand in the back and wait for the moment when they come forward to participate. They don't understand fully, but they see in part what they will one day see fully," Lee says. He described a young boy whose family had not been accustomed to attending worship. The congregation taught him to take a generous piece of bread rather than a small pinch of it. "They talked about the bread of heaven, Christ nurturing us. He took a big piece of bread, and everyone celebrated with the boy, who took a substantial piece of bread with him as he left the station. He wasn't eating because he was hungry, but because he 'got it.'"

At Lake Travis Church, where Laura and Chuck Mendenhall serve, the half dozen or so children under the age of eight or ten commune with everyone else. Laura says, "It means they're part of it. They're not set aside in any way as not yet big enough to be 'church' . . . They bring the offering forward." Chuck adds, "We haven't done a lot of instruction about this. The sense is that it's in the doing of it that they begin to experience it."

Moderator Neal Presa hears children wondering, when they gather and see no bread or cup on the Table yet, "Where is it?" He uses almost every children's sermon to catechize them about the Sacraments. At Faith Church in Colorado Springs, Tom Trinidad, the Vice Moderator, believes it is appropriate for children to share in the financial offering, the prayers, and the Eucharist. "I often talk about the Table in the children's message," he says.

When members of the congregation of First Church in Tallahassee were writing letters to the Session reflecting on their experience with weekly Eucharist, one person wrote, "As someone who lives much of my life with young children, I watch with wonder as Daniel, Amy, Lillian, Katie, Sam, Christopher, Emma, Nathan, Matthew, Zoe, Luke, Sarah, Andrew, Eleanor, and all the other baptized children participate fully and enthusiastically at the table in the weekly act of thanksgiving and worship. How could we explain to them that there is now a calendar which means that they are not welcomed by Jesus to eat and drink and be blessed today?" And another letter said, "I grew up in a tradition that did not baptize infants or celebrate the Eucharist. Believers' Baptism was the creed while the Lord's Supper was a memorial observed rarely more than quarterly . . . For the last year I have been privileged to sit at the Lord's Table on a weekly basis. I see the joy in my children's faces as they celebrate the Eucharist."[1]

Chip Andrus, reporting from the South Salem Church, believes that even the children see a connection between being fed and going out to feed others. "They look forward to Communion. They come forward and

1. Copeland, *Eucharist*, 17.

are very serious about it. I think they're finding that they're able to be in the service with everybody else and doing something with everybody else. They can even be models to others—a child will eagerly come up and show a newcomer how the process works."

Sacramental Catechesis

The congregations that have instituted weekly Eucharist have typically done a good deal of instruction as part of their project of critiquing practice and presenting a vision for recovering an old practice made new. Some continue to interpret weekly Communion even when the practice has grown familiar, both to help members deepen their understanding of why they do it and to familiarize visitors or potential new members with the study and reflection that has led the congregation to the commitment it has made.

When the West Plano Church faced criticism of its Communion practices from a few who had found them quite unlike their experience in previous churches, and even the Session included some who were relatively new to the church, knowing little of the congregation's history and development, Pastor David Batchelder prepared a handout for the Session addressing some of the criticisms. He spoke to questions such as, What does it mean to be Presbyterian? and, how did this church decide that it would take this way of expressing the Reformed tradition? The Worship and Music committee did some research that included looking at worship aids used in past years at West Plano that reflected its liturgical and Sacramental development. The committee concluded that who they are and what they have become grows out of what they believe they were called to be, and want to be. They prepared a series of slides to report their findings, and the Session was so impressed with it that they added the slide show to the church's website. Batchelder believes that the church "must continually revisit its story of how it came to make the decisions it made that provided it with an identity that is still not the most common in the denomination, because there are many ways it gets contested and challenged."

At Faith Church in Colorado Springs, Pastor Tom Trinidad describes some classes that addressed the question, why weekly Communion? They look directly at the pattern evident in Scripture, explicitly in the book of Acts, and they reflected also on the meal practices of Jesus, and on the postresurrection meal in the Emmaus story recorded in Luke 24.

Explicit catechesis has not seemed necessary, for the most part, at the Lake Travis Church, where Pastor Laura Mendenhall believes that people who are new to the church become used to weekly Communion from the beginning. "It doesn't seem extraneous. We don't stop and explain what we're doing, but in the way we go about the whole liturgy, it just sort of flows and people seem to move with it." When called upon to explain the practice, they are happy to do it. A recent new member had been Clerk of Session in another congregation, and she was curious about the practice at Lake Travis. Chuck and Laura explained it to her, and she got it.

The congregation Elizabeth Deibert serves, Peace Church in Lakewood Ranch, Florida, has a paragraph in the bulletin every Sunday that explains the unity of Word and Sacrament, the use of inclusive language in worship, and other features of the worship service. Deibert explains how that congregation offers an annual Sunday school class for children and youth of all ages to teach about the meaning of the Sacrament. She also observes that her congregation appeals to former Roman Catholics, who make up about one-third of the Session. "For them, it's not foreign. The fact that we're having the Sacrament is perhaps what kept them coming. Those who had belonged to various Protestant traditions occasionally ask 'why' on a first visit, but after worshiping with us for several Sundays, they come to appreciate the consistency of a weekly Sacramental service." Russell Sullivan, pastor of Pine Street in Harrisburg, believes that weekly Eucharist can have an evangelistic aspect to it. He adds, "I have never heard a negative comment from a visitor or a new member about why we do this. Not even from lifelong Presbyterians."

Fred Anderson, at Madison Avenue, finds that times with the children (called children's sermons in some churches) have become marvelous occasions for sacramental education, not only for the children, but also for adults who are listening in. Of course, Calvin thought of it first. He discovered in his own pastoral ministry how useful it was for children to become the teachers of the congregation. In Geneva, children learned to sing the Psalms, then taught the congregation, who, like congregations today, may be readier to learn a new thing from children than from grown-up authorities.

Russell Sullivan, from Harrisburg, notes that both he and the church's music director like to teach worship, "and the Eucharistic Prayer is a great resource for teaching worship." That prayer, the Great Thanksgiving, serves well as a structural outline for teaching basic Bible and basic theology as well as worship, whether for new or longtime members, beginning with its tripartite, Trinitarian structure.

In Tallahassee, Brant Copeland expressed special delight as he recalled the church's most recent confirmation class, whose members have grown up hearing the gospel story rehearsed in the Great Thanksgiving most Sundays. "They know the general outlines of the biblical narrative. We asked them to define basic Christian vocabulary: Eucharist, Lord's Supper, Trinity, salvation, prophecy—their answers were not seminary answers, but very solid; and quite affirming for Christy [Williams, the church's Christian educator] and me was that they had learned this through life in the community . . . They have a broader notion of this classic Christian vocabulary than many of their parents do."

At Edgewood Church in Birmingham, Alabama, Sid Burgess, the pastor, visits the sanctuary before the start of the service, identifies newcomers, introduces himself and offers a brief interpretation of the church's practice. After worship, a lay leader in the church pulls together a few chairs and conducts a postservice Worship Reflection class set up in the narthex, where coffee and doughnuts are served. The location poses no difficulty for newcomers to find, and they know from the beginning what the discussion will be about. Having just attended worship, they will have impressions to bring to the conversation. This proves to be an excellent starting point.

Use of Space

While most congregations find ways to use existing space to engage a more energetic sacramental practice, some have made either large or small changes in the physical environment to accent Baptism and Eucharist. At Owensboro, First Presbyterian Church, in response to suggestions made in *Invitation to Christ*, brought its baptismal font from a corner and placed it in the center aisle right in front of the steps that lead to the Communion Table in the chancel. They have taken the top off it and fill it with fresh water every day. Communicants often touch the water as they approach the Table. Soon they will have a new font now being designed and constructed, in which water will be flowing all the time. At Owensboro and at Peace Church, and certainly also in very many Presbyterian congregations, water is poured into the font at some point before the Prayer of Confession or at the Declaration of Forgiveness, evoking the Sacrament of Baptism in both sound and sight.

Owning the Practice

West Plano Presbyterian Church has also placed its baptismal font near the middle of the sanctuary, in a broad center aisle, situated on an octagonal design on the floor. (Traditionally, fonts were fashioned in an octagonal shape, representing both the eighth day of creation—the Lord's Day—and the eight human beings carried to safety in Noah's ark.) When people come to the Table to commune, they encounter the font. Nearly everyone touches the water and makes the sign of the cross, a reminder that they are baptized. As the two Sacraments surely belong together, West Plano is careful to lift up their connection boldly.

The Edgewood Church moved the Lord's Table from the chancel to the floor level, replacing a solid, altar-like one with another that is recognizably a Table. The baptismal font, which had been stuck between the wall and a piano, was moved into a prominent position near the Table. They created a dedicated space for the Table and another for the font, marking them by the use of hardwood flooring in a sanctuary that is otherwise carpeted, visibly linking the two Sacraments.

At Middlesex Presbyterian Church, where Neal Presa serves as pastor, the baptismal font was moved into the center aisle. The pews are moveable, and were arranged in a square. The Table was moved from the chancel to the middle of the assembly. In this church, copies of the *Book of Common Worship* are available in the pews.

Madison Avenue Church experienced a crisis that led to an opportunity. On a Saturday morning, a large portion of plaster fell from the ceiling into the sanctuary. The need to make urgent repairs led to a twelve-million-dollar capital campaign to refurbish and remodel the sanctuary. This required relocating the worship services to a Parish Hall for a time, and then to a second-floor gym. In those settings, the congregation was able to arrange the spaces in ways that allowed them to experience worship in a more intimate way. This led to decisions about the sanctuary renovation, which resulted in a Table that is central, thrusting into the nave, and in a waist-high, solid marble baptismal font, large enough for immersing an infant, situated in the crossing in front of the Table.

At Lake Travis, their new building provides space for the font, Table, and pulpit on a small bema, elevated just one step up from floor level for the sake of visibility. The Table occupies the center position, with the font and pulpit on either side of it. All three pieces have been made by two members of the congregation. Other than a paschal candle, there will be no chairs or any other furnishings on the bema, according to Pastor Laura Mendenhall, freeing these central symbols to make their statements without distractions.

Enough Bread and Some to Share

In Tallahassee, Brant Copeland believes that the congregation discerns a link between the Table spread before the assembly and service to the community, "because every Sunday we serve a meal to people struggling with homelessness." A local social-service agency organizes the meal, and the church hosts it, while various other churches and groups take turns serving the meal, including First Presbyterian. "What we've started doing is, instead of the standard TV dinner kinds of meals provided by the social-service agency, we're serving 'church food'—casseroles, etc. Instead of sitting at long tables, they sit at round tables, and people from the congregation sit with them and just chat. People are beginning to make the connection between the meal and the feeding of the hungry. We also have a garden in the church courtyard for mentally handicapped people to use to raise food." Copeland asks himself whether the congregation would still be committed to social justice issues or hunger issues if they didn't have Communion every Sunday. He reflects, "I do think that it serves that commitment, but there's no way to measure it."

Chip Andrus at South Salem comments about their weekly Eucharist,

> But now we're seeing how to understand the Eucharist as eating with the risen Christ who binds us together and sends us out in service. We're being nourished at the Table to go out and feed others—literally and metaphorically. The emphasis on mission in this church has just exploded—and I attribute that to Word and Sacrament. The church is your whole life, not just a once-a-week affair. The extension of the Table is represented by the presence of a food bank here. The people begin to get these connections. And, we have a fellowship hour after every worship service... We bring the Communion bread to the fellowship hour.

At Madison Avenue, a meal is served every Thursday night to 175 people, in a consortium with other churches and synagogues. "We operate a shelter that houses a dozen homeless men every night and we feed them; and we have a partnership with the Yorkville Common Pantry, which is a huge corporation that is supported by all the churches and synagogues in New York City, and in the Yorkville area gives out food to the poor and hungry and needy. We tend to have shopping carts in the narthex... and people are accustomed to bringing food to put in them." Madison Avenue was, from very early on, one of the churches associated with the Social Gospel movement, and that shapes their identity. They were the founders of the

Neighborhood Coalition for Shelter. "Worship, preaching, and mission are all united at Madison Avenue Presbyterian Church," Pastor Fred Anderson observes.

Upper Room Fellowship in Pittsburgh, as a new congregation, has fewer resources than a large, established church, but it also has a sense of mission. For now, they have decided that the most effective thing they can do is to partner with existing organizations in the city. Upper Room works with the Pittsburgh Region International Student Ministry (PRISM), which reaches more internationals in the city than any other organization known to the pastors. Every Sunday evening, the organization hosts a hospitality night in a local church, which involves providing a meal and conversational partners for international guests, and Upper Room takes its turn. Now Upper Room is creating a deacons' ministry to provide neighborhood-assistance work responding to people who need help paying rent or buying groceries.

Laura Mendenhall sees the Table in the Lake Travis Church becoming "a place of welcome for everyone and the place of our outreach. We bring food once a month for a homeless shelter, and we put it underneath the Communion Table. And once a month people bring clothes and shoes, and it's a really powerful image of who we are as God's people. We come here to be fed, and we feed others." A woman in the congregation is weaving a basket that will be placed permanently beneath the Table in the new church to receive these gifts.

The West Plano Church also collects food once a month in relationship to the Lord's Supper, and the food is blessed at the end of the service and carried out. This congregation understands the Sacraments to help them lead more human lives. "What it means is to take seriously the lives we live in these bodies, treasuring them. Incarnational theology underlies the Sacraments," says David Batchelder, "so the Sacraments connect us to the whole of the material world, our neighbors who have bodies, this earth. Everything about caring for life (bodily life) is feeding people, healing, the issue of homelessness."[2] West Plano has a community garden called Jeremiah's Plot, and there are plots dedicated to the food pantry for which the church tithes 10 percent. They work with Family Promise, an interfaith homeless network, taking turns housing families who have nowhere else to go. With Dallas Interfaith Network, they work on social-justice issues related, for example, to undocumented people, to people who are uninsured,

---

2. See also Batchelder, "Sacramental Liturgy."

to securing voting rights, and so forth. They are known for being a hands-on church.

Pine Street in Harrisburg, where they have been celebrating weekly Communion for more than twenty years, has a soup kitchen called Downtown Daily Bread, where they serve a meal every day and provide other services for homeless persons or for anyone who needs them. Russell Sullivan quotes Dick Adams, a predecessor as pastor at Pine Street, who used to say, "We cannot eat at this Table until we've fed people at the other table." Adams always made a connection between eating at the Lord's Table and feeding people who are hungry in the world. "People sense that here," Sullivan says.

Jim Walker, one of the pastors of the Hot Metal Bridge Faith Community in Pittsburgh, declares that "our church is a kind of outreach. It's a 'mission trip' all the time." From the beginning, they provided a Saturday lunch for homeless people. At first they prepared the meal in the basement of a tattoo shop. "Instead of just dropping off the meals, we would take them to the homeless people and sit down and eat with them . . . We probably know every homeless person in the city pretty well." One of them, named Al, was alcoholic. Al lived on a cement slab beneath a railroad bridge. He became involved with HMB.

> He got off of alcohol, found a job, found a place to live. And now Al runs the homeless ministry at the church. He knows all the homeless people, so on Saturday we gather (anyone is welcome to come, and we have people from other churches), and Al sends them around to different homeless camps, and they sit and get to know the homeless people for a while, and connect in that way. And people who live in poverty or who are nearly homeless are part of our church—not just "projects" to "fix." The homeless people are involved in leadership. We have homeless working in the kitchen and leading worship and leading prayer.

In Memphis, the members of Idlewild feed the hungry and invite them to share the Holy Table as well. In Lexington, Kentucky, Second Presbyterian Church and an army of volunteers continues to prepare and deliver meals every weekday, having initiated Meals on Wheels in Lexington in 1969, well before establishing their early service of Word and Sacrament in 1983. Certainly, these Presbyterian congregations that celebrate weekly Eucharist in their principal service or in another are not unique in their commitment to feed the hungry. Many others are equally committed to feeding ministries. The congregations for whom Word and Sacrament together are the norm every Sunday, however, enjoy the possibility of being able to discern a clearer link between the Table at which Jesus Christ dines with us and nourishes us and the everyday, embodied lives of human beings who need food and drink to sustain life itself. Those who know themselves as needing to be fed are privileged to share in the duty and delight of helping others to be fed.

Both Judaism and Christianity, each in its own way, are meal-keeping faiths, and the gospel also calls the people of God to be a meal-sharing movement, both in response to immediate need and as a sign of the promise of the Messianic banquet. Luke records Mary's song, the Magnificat, in which she rejoices that God "has filled the hungry with good things" (Luke 1:53), and in his Sermon on the Mount Jesus blesses "you who are hungry now, for you will be filled" (Luke 6:21). Eucharist both addresses our own hunger and leads us toward other hungry people.

Bibliography

Anderson, Fred R. "Moving toward Every Sunday Communion." Parts 1, 2, 3, 4, http://arlw.org/ Newsletters: Fall 2006, Spring 2007, Fall 2007, Spring 2008.

Andrus, Chip. "Moving to Weekly Eucharist: A Pastoral Perspective." *Call to Worship: Liturgy, Music, Preaching, and the Arts* 46/2 (2012) 35–38.

Batchelder, David. "Sacramental Liturgy and Its Continuing Incarnation in Mission." *Call to Worship: Liturgy, Music, Preaching, and the Arts* 44/4 (2011) 1–9.

Barth, Karl. *The Preaching of the Gospel*. Translated by B. E. Hook. Philadelphia: Westminster, 1963.

Calvin, John. *Institutes of the Christian Religion*. Edited by John T. McNeill. 2 vols. Library of Christian Classics 20–21. Philadelphia: Westminster, 1960.

Childs, Brevard S. *The Book of Exodus: A Critical, Theological Commentary*. Old Testament Library. Philadelphia: Westminster, 1974.

Christian Reformed Church. *Psalter Hymnal: All Song Texts*. Grand Rapids: CRC Publications, 1997–1998.

Copeland, Brant S. *Eucharist and Resurrection*. Unpublished manuscript.

Dawn, Marva. *Reaching Out without Dumbing Down: A Theology of Worship for the Turn-of-the-Century Culture*. Grand Rapids: Eerdmans, 1995.

Episcopal Church. *The Book of Common Prayer and Administration of the Sacraments and Other Rites and Ceremonies of the Church according to the Use of the Protestant Episcopal Church in the United States of America* (1928). New York: The Church Pension Fund, 1945.

———. *The Book of Common Prayer and Administration of the Sacraments and Other Rites and Ceremonies of the Church according to the use of the Episcopal Church*. New York: The Church Hymnal Corporation, 1979.

Evangelical Lutheran Church in America. *Evangelical Lutheran Worship*. Minneapolis: Augsburg Fortress, 2006.

———. *Principles for Worship*. Renewing Worship 2. Minneapolis: Augsburg Fortress, 2002.

———. *The Use of the Means of Grace: A Statement on the Practice of Word and Sacrament*. Minneapolis: Augsburg Fortress, 1997.

Gerrish, B. A. *Grace and Gratitude: The Eucharist in John Calvin's Theology*. Minneapolis: Fortress, 1993.

Gladwell, Malcolm. *The Tipping Point: How Little Things Can Make a Big Difference*. Boston: Back Bay Books, 2002.

Hageman, Howard G. *Pulpit and Table: Some Chapters in the History of Worship in the Reformed Churches*. Richmond: John Knox, 1962.

Hawn, C. Michael. *Gather into One: Praying and Singing Globally*. Grand Rapids: Eerdmans, 2003.

Bibliography

Hopson, Hal H. *Communion Songs: Cantor, Congregation, and Keyboard, with opt. Flute and Choir*. Fenton, MO: Morningstar Music, 2007.

Jungmann, Joseph A., SJ. *The Mass of the Roman Rite: Its Origins and Development*. New rev. and abridged ed. New York: Benziger, 1959.

Lathrop, Gordon W. *The Four Gospels on Sunday: The New Testament and the Reform of Christian Worship*. Minneapolis: Fortress, 2012.

Lutheran Church in America. *Lutheran Book of Worship*. Prepared by the churches participating in the Inter-Lutheran Commission on Worship. Minneapolis: Augsburg, 1978.

Miles, Sara. *Take This Bread: A Radical Conversion*. New York: Ballantine, 2008.

Moore-Keish, Martha L. *Do This in Remembrance of Me: A Ritual Approach to Reformed Eucharistic Theology*. Grand Rapids: Eerdmans, 2008.

Presbyterian Church (USA). *Book of Common Worship*. Louisville: Westminster John Knox, 1993.

———. *Clerk's Annual Questionnaire for Year Ending December 31, 2012: Survey Questions and Responses*, http://www.pcusa.org/site_media/media/uploads/research/pdfs/caq2012-sqar.pdf/.

———. *Glory to God: The Presbyterian Hymnal*. Louisville: Westminster John Knox, 2013.

———. *Holy Is the Lord: Music for Lord's Day Worship*. Louisville: Geneva, 2002.

———. *Invitation to Christ: A Guide to Sacramental Practices*. Font and Table. Louisville: Presbyterian Church (USA), on behalf of the Office of Theology and Worship, 2006, http://www.pcusa.org/resource/invitation-christ/.

———. *The Service for the Lord's Day: The Worship of God*. Supplemental Liturgical Resource 1. Philadelphia: Westminster, 1984.

———, Research Services. "Sacramental Practices of Congregations." Louisville: Presbyterian Church (USA) Research Services, 2011.

———, Research Services. *Session Annual Statistical Report Supplement End of Year 1997: A Summary of the Research Data Received through the Clerk's Annual Questionnaire*. Louisville: Presbyterian Church (USA), 1998.

———, Research Services. *Session Annual Statistical Report Supplement End of Year 2004: A Summary of the Research Data Received through the Clerk's Annual Questionnaire*, Louisville: Presbyterian Church (USA), 2006.

Sataline, Suzanne. "Church Uses Drama to Draw New Crowd: Pastors with Tattoos." Reprinted from the *Wall Street Journal* on *Pittsburgh Post-Gazette.com*, April 14, 2006. Online: http://www.post-gazette.com/lifestyle/2006/04/14/Church-uses-drama-to-draw-new-crowd-pastors-with-tattoos/stories/200604140116/.

Schmemann, Alexander. *Introduction to Liturgical Theology*. 1966. 4th printing. Crestwood, NY: St. Vladimir's Seminary Press, 1996.

Thompson, Bard. *Liturgies of the Western Church*. Philadelphia: Fortress, 1961.

United Presbyterian Church in the USA. Directory for the Worship of God, in *The Constitution of The United Presbyterian Church in the United States of America, Part II, The Book of Order*. New York: Office of the General Assembly of the United Presbyterian Church in the United States of America, 1961.

Volf, Miroslav. "Proclaiming the Lord's Death." *The Christian Century*, March 3, 1999, 253.

Wainwright, Geoffrey. *Eucharist and Eschatology*. Akron, OH: OSL Publications, 2002.

White, James F. *A Brief History of Christian Worship*. Nashville: Abingdon, 1993.

Names Index

Adams, Dick, 124
Al, 4, 124
A Statement of Communion Practices, 107
Anderson, Fred, xv, 4, 20, 27, 43, 54, 56, 59, 60, 63, 67, 72, 76, 77–79, 82–84, 86, 115, 119, 123, 127
Andrus, Charles xv, 3, 20, 86–90, 92, 117, 122, 127
Anglican, 24, 42, 109
Augsburg Confession, 108
Augustine, 49
Austin Presbyterian Seminary, 9, 21, 22
Austin, Texas, 7, 9, 10, 21, 22, 43, 47, 61, 70, 71, 116

Babette's Feast, 90
Baptist, 3, 6–9, 19–21, 26
Barth, Karl, 19, 36, 39, 127
Batchelder, David, xv, 5, 20, 21, 57, 93, 94, 115, 118, 123, 127
Birmingham, Alabama, 6, 21, 68, 114, 116, 120
Blake, Eugene Carson, 48
Book of Common Prayer, xvi, 106, 107, 109, 127
Book of Common Worship, ix, xvi, 2, 35, 36, 39, 45, 53, 61, 65, 71, 81, 110, 111, 121, 128
Book of Confessions, 49
Book of Order, 2, 21, 113, 128
Brown, Christopher, 12, 22
Brown, Robert McAfee, 36

Buchanan, John, 102
Burgess, John, 22
Burgess, Sidney, xv, 6, 7, 21, 95, 116, 120
Buttrick, George, 3, 82

Calvin College and Calvin Theological Seminary, xi
Calvin, John, 19, 20, 21, 28, 33–36, 45, 47, 49, 51, 53, 55, 57, 60, 77, 109, 111, 119, 127
Central College, 19
Carroll, Jonathan, xv, 4, 89, 91, 92
Central Washington Presbytery, 18
Chalcedon, 50
Chicago, Illinois, 68, 98, 102
Christian Reformed Church, 60, 69, 127
Church of England, 109
Church of Scotland, 24, 46
Church of the Savior, 14
Church of the Servant, 60, 62
Clark-Jones, Thomas, 61
Coffin, Henry Sloane, 82
Colorado Springs, Colorado, 2, 4, 19, 42, 61, 92, 117, 118
Columbia Seminary 10, 21
Confession of 1967, 50
Copeland, Brant, xv, 7, 24, 25, 39, 54, 56, 67, 80–82, 116, 117, 120, 122, 127
Corzine, Michael, 67
Council of Trent, 57

Names Index

Covenant Community Presbyterian Church, 13, 14, 23, 69, 98, 100
Covenant Presbyterian Church, 9
Cranmer, Thomas, 109

Daily Prayer, 87
Davies, Horton, 20
Dawn, Marva, 39, 127
Deibert, Elizabeth, xv, 8, 9, 17, 21, 22, 28, 42, 65, 69, 116, 119
Deibert, Richard, 21
Directory for Worship, xvi, 2, 4, 20, 21, 36, 37, 39, 55, 64, 65, 71, 73, 77, 95, 110, 128
Dowey, Edward, 20
Downtown Daily Bread, 124
Duba, Arlo, 20

Eddings, Jeff, 15, 44
Edgewood Presbyterian Church, 6, 7, 21, 68, 70, 95, 114, 116, 120, 121
Emmaus, 31, 42, 53, 87, 118
Enlightenment, xiv, 24, 27, 32–34, 37, 38, 50
Episcopal (Episcopalian), 8, 30, 36, 42, 99, 100, 105–7, 109, 111, 127
Evangelical Lutheran Church in America (ELCA), xvi, 36, 107–9, 127
Evangelical Lutheran Worship, xvi, 108–110, 127

Faith Presbyterian Church, 2–4, 19, 42, 61, 92, 93, 117, 118
Farel, Guillaume, 34
Farwell, James, 106
First Presbyterian Church
  Birmingham, Michigan, v
  Colorado Springs, Colorado, 19
  Harrison, Arkansas, 3
  Lake Forest, Illinois, 98, 100

Lexington, Kentucky, 66
Owensboro, Kentucky 4, 58, 61, 68, 91, 120
Tallahassee, Florida, 7, 24, 39, 67, 80, 81, 116, 117, 122
Formula Missae, 109
Fourth Presbyterian Church, 102, 103
Fronczek, Adam, xv, 102

Gambrell, David, xv
Gayton Kirk, 103
Gehrling, Michael, xv, 12, 13, 22
Genesis Presbyterian Church, 9
Gerrish, Brian, 45, 127
Gladwell, Malcolm, 112, 127
Glasgow, Scotland, 46
Glory to God, 9, 110, 128
Grand Rapids, Michigan, xi, 60, 62, 127, 128
(Great) Thanksgiving, 9, 32, 39, 45, 69–71, 81, 119, 120

Hadaway, C. Kirk, 105
Hageman, Howard, 40, 42, 127
Hall, Stan, 9, 22
Harrisburg, Pennsylvania, 4, 20, 43, 56, 62, 63, 76, 84, 119, 124
Harrison, Arkansas, 3, 20, 71, 86, 87, 89
Hawn, Michael, 68, 127
Hendrix, T. Judson (Jud), xv, 13, 14, 23, 69, 98
Henrico, Virginia, 103
Homewood, Alabama, 6
Hopson, Hal, 69, 128
Hot Metal Bridge Faith Community (HMB), 15, 16, 23, 28, 43, 44, 69, 124
Hotz, Kendra, 101
Hudson River Presbytery, 88

Idlewild Presbyterian Church, 53, 100, 101, 124

Names Index

Immanuel Presbyterian Church, 8, 21, 22
Invitation to Christ, 18, 63, 91, 120, 128
Iona, 46, 47

James, Janet, 103
James Lees Memorial Presbyterian Church, 14
Jesuits, 46, 47
Justin Martyr, 32, 45

Kaznak, Elizabeth, 13
Knox, John, 24, 35, 57, 109, 127, 128

Lackey, Wes, 6
Lake Forest College, 98
Lake Forest, Illinois, 97, 98, 100
Lake Travis Presbyterian Church, 10, 43, 61, 68, 71, 117, 119, 121, 123
Lakeway, 10
Lakewood Ranch, Florida, 8, 22, 61
Lathrop, Gordon, 30, 31, 107, 128
Latrobe Presbyterian Church, 5
Lee, James, xv, 9, 10, 17, 22, 28, 43, 47, 116, 117
Lewisboro, New York, 86
Lexington, Kentucky, v, 61, 66, 73, 96, 124
Louisville, Kentucky, 13, 14, 20, 23, 69, 98, 128
Louisville Seminary, 20
Luckey, Ronald, 107
Luther, Martin, 33, 34
Lutheran, xvi, 8, 19, 33, 34, 36, 51, 62, 100, 105, 107–11, 127, 128
Lutheran Book of Worship (LBW), xvi, 107, 109, 110

MacLeod, George, 46, 47
Madison Avenue Presbyterian Church, 3, 4, 20, 27, 43, 64, 67, 68, 82–86, 115, 119, 121–23
Meadows, Betty, 13
Memphis, Tennessee, 24, 53, 100, 101, 124
Mendenhall, Charles, xv, 10, 11, 22, 43, 61, 117, 119
Mendenhall, Laura, xv, 10, 11, 22, 61, 117, 119, 121, 123
Methodists (see also United Methodists) 6, 8, 72
Mid-Kentucky Presbytery, 13
Middlesex, New Jersey, 1–3, 18, 62, 121
Middlesex Presbyterian Church, 1, 3, 18, 62, 121
Miles, Sara, 99, 128
Moderator, xv, 1, 18, 28, 45, 62, 78, 117
Montgomery, Alabama, 8, 21, 22
Montgomery, Stephen, xv, 53, 100, 101
Moore-Keish, Martha, 53, 65, 128
Morning Prayer, 87, 105–7

Nelson, Corey, xv, 97–99
New Covenant Fellowship, 9, 22, 43, 47, 116
New York, New York, 1, 3, 82, 115, 122
New Yorker magazine, 112
Nicaea, 50
Niebuhr, Reinhold, 36

Old, Hughes Oliphant, 19
Orthodox, 19, 51
Owensboro, Kentucky, 4, 58, 120

PCUSA, xvi, 1, 2, 4–8, 15, 18, 28, 37, 38, 48, 98, 101, 103, 104, 107–13, 128
Peace Presbyterian Church, 8, 22, 42, 61, 65, 116, 119, 120
Pella, Iowa, 19

Names Index

Pine Street Presbyterian Church, 4, 20, 43, 56, 60–64, 67, 72, 76, 77, 79, 80, 82, 84, 85, 119, 124
Pittsburgh, Pennsylvania, 11–13, 15, 22, 23, 43, 61, 69, 102, 123, 124, 128
Pittsburgh Presbytery, 11, 12
Pittsburgh Seminary, 12, 15
Presa, Neal, xv, 1, 18, 19, 28, 62, 63, 117, 121
Presa, Grace, 63
Presbyterian Panel, 111, 112
Princeton Seminary, 18–20
Puritan, Puritanism, 34, 73, 109

Read, David H. C., 82, 83
Reformed, ii, ix, xiv, 8, 9, 14, 19, 21, 30, 31, 34, 35, 37, 40–43, 46, 48–51, 53, 57, 68, 70, 72, 84, 91, 95, 100, 102, 109–11, 118, 128
Reformed Church in America, 19, 40
Rhodes College, 24, 101
Roman Catholic, 1, 7–9, 19, 24, 35, 52, 57, 58, 65, 101, 115, 119, 128
Sacraments Study Group, 18, 19
San Francisco, California, 99
San Francisco Seminary, 18
Schmemann, Alexander, 20, 128
Schweitzer, Carol, 58
Scotland, 20, 24, 35, 46, 52, 56
Scottish, 35, 46, 80, 109
Second Presbyterian Church, v, 61, 96, 124
Service Book and Hymnal, 110
Service for the Lord's Day (SLD), xvi, 2, 5, 36, 61, 110, 111, 128
Sewickley, Pennsylvania, 102
Sluka, Jason, 44
Social Gospel, 122
South Salem Presbyterian Church, 20, 71, 86, 88–90, 117, 122

Squirrel Hill, 12, 13, 22, 23
St. Andrews University, 24, 56
St. Giles Cathedral, 62
St. Gregory of Nyssa, 99
Stricklen, Teresa, xv
Sullivan, Russell, xv, 4, 43, 61, 119, 124

Taizé, 68, 70, 99
Tallahassee, Florida, 7, 24, 67, 68, 70, 80, 85, 116, 117, 120, 122
Theological Declaration of Barmen, 50
Trinidad, Thomas, xv, 2, 18, 19, 42, 92, 93, 117, 118

United Methodist Church, 8, 15, 16, 36
Union Presbyterian Seminary, xiv, 58, 80
United Church of Christ, 36
University Presbyterian Church, 7
Upper Room Fellowship, 11–13, 22, 23, 61, 62, 69, 123
The Use of the Means of Grace, 108, 127

Vatican Council, 35, 36, 52, 57
Vice Moderator, xv, 2, 18, 19, 42, 92
Virginia Theological Seminary, 106
Volf, Miroslav, 41, 92, 117

Walker, Gayle, 101
Walker, Jim, xv, 15–17, 23, 28, 43, 44, 69, 124
Weaver, John, 68
Wesley, John, 51
West Plano Presbyterian Church, 5, 6, 20, 69, 93, 114, 115, 118, 121, 123
Westminster Assembly, 110
Westminster Confession, 50
Westminster Presbyterian Church, 10, 22

Names Index

White, James, 19, 20, 24, 59, 128
White, Vera, 11, 12, 15
Williams, Christy, 120
Williams, San, 7

Yorkville Common Pantry, 122

Zurich, 34
Zwingli, 34

www.ingramcontent.com/pod-product-compliance
Lightning Source LLC
Chambersburg PA
CBHW020854160426
43192CB00007B/915